PRACTICAL BONSAI

Their Care, Cultivation and Training

PRACTICAL BONSAI

Their Care, Cultivation and Training

Paul Lesniewicz
Hideo Kato

foulsham

London • New York • Toronto • Cape Town • Sydney

foulsham

W. Foulsham & Company Limited
Yeovil Road, Slough, Berkshire, SL1 4JH

ISBN 0-572-01647-6
Copyright 1991 W. Foulsham & Co. Ltd.

German edition published in 1981 by
Th. Knaur Nacht., Munich

Photoset by Typesetting Solutions, Slough, UK
Printed in Hong Kong

CONTENTS

HISTORICAL BACKGROUND

Bonsai, like all trees, are symbols

AT ONE TIME in Europe it was the custom to mark special events, such as the birth of a child, by planting a tree. Under the old village linden or oak tree it was customary for celebrations, dancing and courts of law to take place. So in Europe trees have had an ancient meaning, signifying primeval and primitive life.

Today, as towns and cities continue to expand and less and less room is to be found for trees, suddenly a new interest in bonsai has emerged – for these miniature editions of trees that can be kept in even the most limited space.

A fully grown bonsai is only some 30–70 cm high, but looks exactly like an old tree that has gone through the different seasons of spring, summer, autumn and winter, with sun, storm and snow. Just like its larger, natural counterpart, the bonsai shows the same signs of age through splits in its bark or the way branches hang down.

The word bonsai is Japanese and means 'tree in a bowl', or 'tree planted in a tray' (*bon* = tray or bowl; *sai* = tree or plant). Just as Europeans at one time linked trees with a particular view of life, the intellectual background of bonsai lies in oriental philosophy. The Asiatic view of life attempts to harmonise man and nature, brought about by an empathy with everything that develops and grows. For this reason, in East Asia bonsai are understood as being a link between heaven and earth, between the human and divine. A bonsai enthusiast is not simply interested in tending his plants, but takes time to ponder over them; he lives through the different seasons with them and intervenes creatively and formatively in their growth.

Over here it is largely young people who have discovered bonsai. They grow their bonsai themselves from seeds and young plants or buy them at bonsai centres.

The Chinese origins

These days most bonsai imported into Europe and America come from Japan. However, the origins of the bonsai culture lie in China. Already during the Han dynasty, which lasted from 202 BC until AD 220, Chinese landscape gardeners had begun to miniaturise artificial rock gardens. A legend about the artist Jiangfeng, who was reputed to have possessed magic powers, tells how he was able by enchantment to shrink landscapes with mountains and rocks, trees and rivers, lakes and houses, animals and men all onto a tray. To this day the Chinese have retained a special liking for bonsai landscapes.

Links are already to be seen in a comparison between the Japanese name *bonsai* and the Chinese name *pun-sai*. The latter has the same characters as *bonsai* and thus effectively points to the origin of the Japanese word.

Not only the smallest bonsai landscape but also single bonsai trees can be traced back a long way, in China back to the Ch'in dynasty of AD 265–420. Even before the year 1000 in the Sung dynasty *pun-sai* is described in poetry, and in specialist *pun-sai* literature the training of bonsai is discussed.

For hundreds of years bonsai was a hobby reserved for the Chinese aristocracy. Not until the Ch'in dynasty in the seventeenth century did the population at large begin to occupy itself with bonsai.

The Japanese get to know bonsai

In the Western world bonsai are automatically linked in our thoughts with Japan – quite rightly, as it is from there that most of these little trees now come, and it was from there that the first information on bonsai reached us in the West.

There is a well-known story about a poor samurai who on one bitterly cold winter's night burned his last three beloved bonsai in order to feed the flames of a dying fire for a respected visitor

It is thought that Buddhist monks brought bonsai with them to Japan in the tenth or eleventh century. To them these little trees were holy; they considered them to be religious objects, a link between the divine and the human.

In Japanese history books bonsai receive their first mention in the Kamakura era (1192–1333) and this in the annals of the Kasagura shrine. On pictorial scrolls of the time there are paintings of miniature trees, planted in pots on stands. These scrolls illustrate the ninth to twelfth centuries. It can be assumed that the first bonsai were already to be found at that time in Japan.

It is also known that in the Heian period bonsai were valued as gifts, and brought by Japanese ministers and merchants from China. The early bonsai culture in Japan can also be substantiated by the legend of a samurai who in the year 1383, on a cold winter's night, received a visit from a shogun travelling secretly through the country on tax matters. For such a respected guest the samurai threw his last three beloved bonsai onto the fire: an apricot, a cherry and a pine.

The bonsai culture in Japan was influenced quite decisively by Chu Shun-sui who around 1644 was forced to flee to Japan from China and the Manchu rulers. He brought with him a complete collection of specialist literature on bonsai and spread his knowledge in Japan. In his lifetime the development of an indigenous Japanese bonsai culture began.

In practical terms, up until the beginning of this century bonsai were – as was the case in China – a hobby of the priests and the aristocracy, the samurai. It was not until the present day that the growing of these tiny trees became a pleasant pastime for many more people, and not just a hobby of famous families, who passed on their bonsai from generation to generation.

Although the Portugese, probably some time in the sixteenth century, learned about bonsai in China, bonsai from Japan were not known in the Western world until the turn of the century when the Japanese exhibited their miniature wonder-trees in 1878 at the World Exhibition in Paris and in 1909 in London.

WHAT IS A TYPICAL BONSAI?

Basic bonsai styles

E VERY BONSAI is an individual just like its larger counterpart in nature, where no tree is like another. However, particular kinds of tree develop their own typical styles. An elm, for example, always differs in appearance from a pine. In the cultivation of bonsai, an attempt is made to underline the basic form of a tree so that it looks at least something like the larger, natural one and at the same time expresses our own aesthetic understanding. How much smaller is the bonsai than a tree outside in nature! Despite this, it retains all that is typical of the larger tree. Structure and character are merely condensed in the miniature tree.

Far Eastern culture shows itself in many different areas, as for example in Ikebana, or in watercolour drawings where a strong stylisation closely follows Japanese aesthetic consciousness. Likewise, the Japanese have developed certain basic styles, 14 in all, to which bonsai cultivation conforms. These are perfected, stylised reproductions of nature, based on the way trees grow in Japan and China after exposure to the wind, when clinging by the roots to rocks, or simply as single trees in open countryside, or as groups.

When growing bonsai the Japanese take considerable trouble to come as close as possible to that which is typical in nature without at the same time breaking the individuality of a single tree.

The 14 basic styles are arranged according to specific principles. For example, the main line of a tree is always its trunk, from which its branches grow in a subordinate harmony. Quite naturally three important subordinate lines result, contributing to the whole shape of the tree, giving it form and harmony. Right from the start it is important that these lines are clearly worked out.

In contrast to Europeans, the Japanese avoid every even

Informal upright style

number, except for the number two. Beauty and harmony have for them very little to do with our understanding of symmetry. They particularly avoid the numbers four and six. So four or six trees should never be planted together as a forest group. A forest group consists of seven or nine plants, and the same rules apply to a group as to a single tree with its main line and the different important subordinate lines: only one tree should be prominent, the strongest, providing a focal point around which all the others are arranged.

Certain types of tree, such as the cascading kind, are most effective when grown as single plants. Other species and shapes, such as the upright trees, are most effectively displayed in groups.

The following are the most important styles:

Moyogi – informal upright style

The trunk twists itself in elegant turns that become narrower towards the apex of the tree. The crown of the tree inclines itself a little towards the viewing side. The branches grow out of the bends. The lower third of the tree should be free from branches.

Chokkan – formal upright style

From a strong, regular, upward-tapering trunk the branches grow to form a pyramid shape. The facing side of the trunk remains free of branches; only at its apex do a few small branches turn towards the viewing side.

Shakan – slanting style

In the slanting style the trunk grows diagonally to one side. The branches grow in all directions – except towards the viewing side. This style represents a tree that has been blown over in storms and is now trying slowly to right itself again.

Han-kengai – semi-cascade style

The trunk of the tree is even more strongly inclined than in the *shakan* style. Its tip reaches the level of the edge of

BONSAI

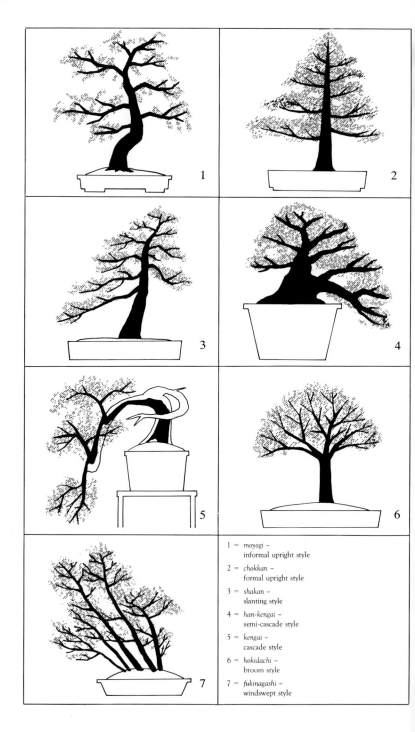

1 = *moyogi* –
   informal upright style

2 = *chokkan* –
   formal upright style

3 = *shakan* –
   slanting style

4 = *han-kengai* –
   semi-cascade style

5 = *kengai* –
   cascade style

6 = *hokidachi* –
   broom style

7 = *fukinagashi* –
   windswept style

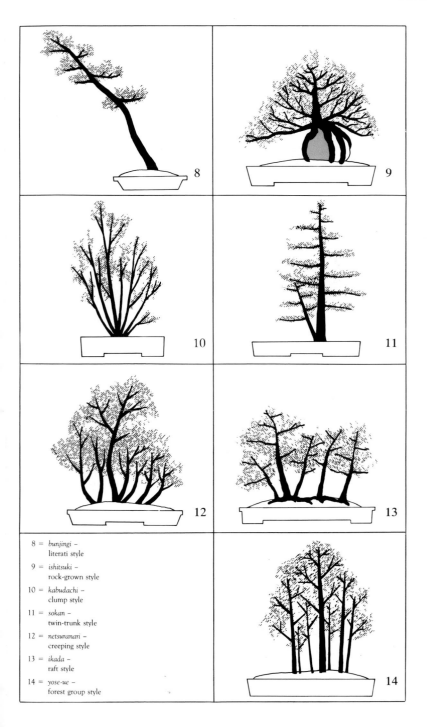

8 = *bunjingi* –
   literati style

9 = *ishitsuki* –
   rock-grown style

10 = *kabudachi* –
   clump style

11 = *sokan* –
   twin-trunk style

12 = *netsuranari* –
   creeping style

13 = *ikada* –
   raft style

14 = *yose-ue* –
   forest group style

the pot and often trails below it. The tree looks as though it has been pressed flat to the ground by wind and weather as it juts out horizontally over a rock or a cliff face.

Kengai – cascade style

The trunk and the branches of the cascade-style tree trail well over the edge of a deep bowl, even falling below its base. For this reason these trees can only be displayed to their best advantage on a high stand. In their natural surroundings these types of tree are to be found hanging over rocks and deep ravines.

Hokidachi – broom style

The *hokidachi* bonsai offers us the well-known picture of an individual tree with an upright trunk, the branches of which only grow from a certain point to form the top of the tree. This style is often compared to a besom.

Fukinagashi – windswept style

In this style the branches and twigs grow on a trunk drawn diagonally in one direction – as though windswept.

Bunjingi – literati style

The literati style portrays those tall pine trees so often found at the edges of woods; a trunk or trunks grow upright or slanting slightly and usually have branches only at the very top of the tree.

Ishitsuki – rock-grown style

There are two kinds of rock bonsai. In the first type, the roots of the tree grow over a lump of rock and into the compost. In the second type, the plant clings by its roots to a rock without touching the soil. In any rock-grown style in which the plants sit on a stone it is normal practice to use a watertight bowl. These bowls are filled with white sand and water.

Zelkova – broom style

Kabudachi – clump style

In this style more than one trunk grows from a single root base. The neck of this root base is almost entirely exposed. This style has been drawn from seeing trees that have had the trunk sawn off near the ground after which several new trunks have grown upwards from the base.

Sokan – twin-trunk style

Two trunks of differing heights and thicknesses grow from one root. Both trunks are grown in such a way as to form an integrated whole.

Netsuranari – creeping style

From a 'creeping' root lying horizontally grow a number of vertical trunks, forming a self-contained unit.

Ikada – raft style

From its appearance the raft style is very much like the creeping style. However, in this case it is a tree rather than a root that is buried, so that its branches appear to be individual trees.

Yose-ue – forest-group style

Trees of different age and height are planted out on a flat tray as a forest group.

All types of woodland scenes can be captured as bonsai forest groups.

Special varieties

Miniature bonsai

Miniature bonsai, known as mame bonsai in Japan, is another variety of Japanese bonsai growing and it has already found many enthusiasts here. In Japan especially, miniature bonsai can change hands for a not insignificant sum amongst connoisseurs and friends of these 'mini-bonsai'. The special thing about the miniature bonsai is its size. Grown to a mere 6–15 cm, it fits neatly and with little difficulty into an open adult hand.

For bonsai enthusiasts with a limited amount of space available this is the ideal plant to collect. Miniature bonsai demand the same rules of care and propagation as normal, larger bonsai; they too should be a reproduction of a natural, fully-grown tree. Although miniature bonsai do not live for several hundred years like the others, with loving care they can survive for many generations. They have the advantage that within only a few years – on the trunk for example – they show the characteristics of a true bonsai.

Practically every small plant suitable for bonsai cultivation can also be used for creating miniature bonsai. Most suitable of all are small-leaved varieties of trees and short-needled pines, but cherry and crab apple trees can also be selected for propagation.

Especially popular are miniature bonsai that carry blossom or fruit. Though these trees do produce fruit and blossom of normal size, they give the appearance of being large due to the smaller proportions of the miniature bonsai. As a rule miniature bonsai are grown from seed or cuttings. Another way of obtaining plants is to collect suitable specimens from the wild in spring, from the woods or mountains, digging them out with great care, trying not to damage the fibrous roots. It is important to remove the taproot right away and to wrap the plant in moss or damp newspaper to prevent it drying out. Then find a suitable pot with a large drainage hole. Specialist shops should be able to offer you suitable pots for miniature bonsai imported from Japan or China. If your prospective 'mini-bonsai' is to survive, it will need the correct compost. A bonsai compost mixture of fine soil and a lot of loam is the most suitable. The worst enemy of a bonsai is dryness. These tiny plants get thirsty up to three times a day. In order that the two or three dessertspoonsful of compost in which they grow does not dry out, the easiest solution is to dip the plant completely in

Japanese white pine – windswept style, 60 years old

Dwarf azalea – slanting style, 50 years old

a water container until air bubbles no longer rise to the surface.

As miniature bonsai are very difficult to wire, regular pruning is the most successful way of achieving the desired shape. In the case of young plants taken from the wild, every shoot, except for one or two buds, should first be cut away. To achieve an interesting shape to the plant it is only necessary to snap off the dominant branches with the fingers, so encouraging growth in the weaker ones. If a mame bonsai with hanging branches is required in the cascade style then the branches must be tied down with threads. To do this the bonsai pot must be tied all over like a parcel using string. Then the branches are wrapped round with thread, pulled downwards as far as possible and fastened tightly to the lacework of string around the pot. Even the tiniest tree needs nutrition. It is best to use a liquid manure, applied when watering from the spring through to the autumn. Before feeding, the compost should already be quite damp. As the compost is quickly exhausted, the tree should, under normal circumstances, be repotted once a year. The roots should then be pruned back by a third. Leaves that have become too large can be completely removed. After repotting the plant needs to be placed in a protected environment for about a week. It should not be exposed to wind or sun.

Indoor bonsai

This is an American term and is used of those bonsai that can be kept indoors throughout the whole year. By contrast all the bonsai mentioned up to now are, and remain, outdoor plants preferring to be outside throughout the year and can only survive a few days at a time indoors. After all, although much smaller than their natural counterparts, they are still trees. One can imagine how a pine tree would react to being suddenly kept indoors. Because many bonsai enthusiasts, both in America and Europe, have neither a garden nor even a balcony, a demand for indoor bonsai has developed – something the Japanese grower does not see the need for, as he does not make the sharp distinction we do between indoors and out.

In America, attempts have already been made to grow indoor bonsai, and in Europe such attempts are only in their early stages. As with the other types of bonsai, drawn from plants growing in the open, all indoor plants having woody stems and small leaves provide suitable plants for indoor bonsai. Tropical varieties requiring no rest in winter, such as small-leaved rubber trees and gardenias, are particularly suitable. However, with these plants new growing styles have still to be developed, as their natural growth style bears little resemblance to the traditional bonsai styles. The temperature for these species must never be allowed to drop below 15°C and they can remain indoors the whole year round. Certain cool greenhouse plants can be grown indoors to look like outdoor trees, such as *Serissa foetida*, myrtle, camellias, the citrus fruits and olive trees.

If they are to thrive indoors such cool greenhouse plants require a climate that approximates as closely as possible, in terms of light, temperature and humidity, to the conditions of their natural environment. It is best to place the plant in a south-facing window if at all possible, but not over a radiator – and to spray it regularly with water. If there is not sufficient natural light, then artificial light should be added. In summer the best place for these plants is in the open, as long as the temperature at night does not fall below 5°C. The place should be sheltered and away from the wind, and in light shadow.

Important for cool greenhouse plants is a difference of temperature between night and day of at least 5°C, especially in winter. If no other way can be found, then the plants can be carried into a cooler room at night or, alternatively, keep the window cooler than the rest of the room by separating it with a thick curtain.

Saikei (miniature Japanese landscapes)

Saikei are small landscapes arranged on trays, looking like miniature copies of natural scenes, such as a running river, a pine grove beside the sea, a lakeside, a section of primeval forest, a secluded deciduous wood with paths and streams, and so on. *Saikei* are planted in shallow trays using different types of compost and studded with stones. They are not the same as the bonsai forest group style. In *saikei* different species of tree, all of different heights, are planted together. Another difference is that not only stones, but also small houses and figures are added.

Saikei (the word comes from *sai* = a plant, the planting of a tree, and *kei* = landscape, prospect) probably have their origins in religious plantings of earlier days. As a popular and successful form of bonsai growing they were developed first after the Second World War by Toshio Kawamoto, an old master of the Japanese bonsai art. As yet *saikei* are rarely seen in Europe, but in Japan they enjoy increasing popularity.

In contrast to *bonkai* – miniature landscapes made largely from artificial materials – *saikei* offer the possibility of using all the expertise gained by growing and caring for bonsai.

What plants and trees are suitable for use in *saikei*?

All those trees that can be grown as bonsai are suitable for *saikei*. However, the trees do not need to be grown to such perfection. Indeed, trees can be used that are perhaps not quite good enough for growing as bonsai. Besides this, *saikei* demands much less patience. Whilst a little tree takes as much as seven years to grow into a respectable bonsai specimen, young trees in a miniature landscape can be planted out when they are just two to four years old. They can be gathered as cuttings or seeds from the wild in the spring. Very often in Japan bonsai are grown from what started off as *saikei* trees.

Unlike the bonsai group style, in *saikei* contrasting

Special bonsai variations are *saikei* – Japanese miniature landscapes. Here is an example of landscape planted with Japanese cedar

varieties of trees in many different growing styles are planted together. The important thing is not to seek to impress with the growing to perfection of an individual tree, but to create a harmonious landscape, looking, as it were, quite 'genuine'.

Saikei differs too from the bonsai rock-grown style, which is characterised by a carefully selected rock-grown plant. On the other hand, it is impossible to imagine *saikei* without rocks or stones. All kinds of stones gathered from the countryside can be used. The only proviso is that the piece of rock or stone should be appropriate to the kind of landscape envisaged. The proportions in *saikei* are determined largely by the rocks. Although they do not need to be perfect, the stones used should really have interesting surfaces. Anything that does not quite fit in to the general concept can be simply covered with compost.

Saikei styles are very similar to bonsai group styles: there are cascades, informal, and formal upright styles. The young plants are treated in the same way as miniature bonsai, pruning leaves and roots and wiring to style them. *Saikei* containers are normally not particularly valuable, being rather conservative and unobtrusive. They are usually rectangular or oval, but should, above all, be quite flat.

Having sought out varieties of plants, stones, composts, mosses and short grasses, the drainage holes of the container must be covered and the trees planted complete with root-ball. The arrangement needs very careful thought. Focal points having a natural effect can be established on an oval container by planting a taller group of trees on the right-hand side of a central line down the length of the bowl, and on the left-hand side a group of shorter ones. Using stones and compost, mountains and valleys, gentle hills and steeply inclined coastlines can be recreated. Attention should be given to making everything appear as natural as possible, and this should determine overall proportions so that the grass of the undergrowth, for example, retains the correct scale in proportion to the trees.

Saikei require the same kind of attention as bonsai trees.

In order to ensure that the plants survive repotting in the spring, initially it is best to keep all plants gathered from the wild in single pots where they can be cared for and then later planted together in groups.

Saikei is a great hobby for everyone who does not want to wait seven years for a bonsai, but who would like to derive some pleasure from growing plants from cuttings and seeds. They are all bonsai in a preparatory state. Just like bonsai, saikei need fresh air and a place in the open. For this reason miniature landscapes can only survive a few days in the house before suffering damage.

Chinese bonsai

It was actually in China that bonsai growing began. Despite this these miniature trees have only relatively recently been seen in the West, and even amongst the Chinese they have only recently been readily available to all – as for example in the large parks of Canton, Shanghai and Peking.

It is possible that the cultivation of bonsai became a largely forgotten art as a result of the various periods of unrest the country has been through during this century. However, individual trees have been hidden away and taken care of in order to save them from destruction.

Now once more in China many of the old traditions are being revived. Bonsai too are being brought from the remotest corners of the nurseries and shown to visitors with immense pride. Many real works of art must have been lost and it is thus more important than ever to look after those remaining.

The old, often very valuable, potted bonsai draw forth and deserve wholehearted wonder. Certainly, these little trees surprise us, though some may even disappoint us. This is largely because our eyes have become accustomed to the sight of the Japanese bonsai we have known for so long. Without realising it, Americans and Europeans have taken over the Japanese bonsai styles and the accompanying feeling for shape. They have hardly developed any ideas of their own, and made little progress towards an original bonsai art.

Because of this Japanese way of looking at things,

Left: Chinese bonsai – sageretia
Above: a detail of the same arrangement in close-up

Chinese bonsai appear unusual to us. The Chinese create bonsai according to the same principles as the Japanese, that is to say, they are orientated after the pattern of what is seen in nature. However, they see things through different eyes and have not worked out their basic styles to quite such perfection as their island neighbours. However, for this reason Japanese bonsai also lose a lot in liveliness and are sometimes nothing more than an aesthetic, balanced, but somewhat cold piece of art, whereas Chinese bonsai is not so stylised and consequently they radiate more warmth, more individuality. This does lead now and then to a disharmony and resultant unnaturalness, because roots, trunk and branches are out of proportion with each other, or large swellings on the trunks spoil them. They are then not more natural than their more noble Japanese relations, but simply somewhat more rough and ready.

This could be due to the tools used. The various kinds of ingenious tool available in Japan are hardly seen in China. A pair of pliers has to make do for every job – and so large swellings, that do not arise with a concave branch cutter, cannot be avoided.

In addition, the Chinese like to plant their bonsai in what are often expensive pots, without – unlike the Japanese – placing too much emphasis on the balance between the pot and the height of the plant. Very often Chinese bonsai grow to a height of 1 – 1½ metres. The Chinese bonsai may have what the Japanese would see as a strong trunk in relation to a sometimes rather thin root-base, and also trunks that hardly taper upwards towards the apex – all unthinkable in Japanese bonsai. Thin branches on thick trunks and fine twigs only in the crown strengthen this strange appearance. Daring slanting angles between trunk and branches surprise the viewer.

However, we must not forget that the Chinese tree styles are different to those of Japan and to our own. Landscapes in China have their own peculiarities; and if the natural pattern is different, so bonsai styles will also be different. This applies as much to the plants we know, but equally as much to the subtropical trees and shrubs of South China which can also be grown as bonsai: bougainvillea, rubber trees, gardenias, orange trees, jasmine, *Sageretia thea,* serissa – just to name some of the most important. These are all good bonsai plants, many of which can be grown as indoor bonsai in our climate.

It must also not be forgotten that during the course of centuries the art of bonsai in China has passed through a number of stylistic phases, inspired not so much from natural patterns as from other sources. There was the pagoda style from Yangchow, the style of the dancing dragon from Anwhei region and the five-trunk bonsai particularly popular in Kwangtung province.

It was not until around 1900 that bonsai growers in Kwangtung developed the *lingnan* method, in the West popularly known as 'let it grow – cut it back'. It is a style that coincides with our own understanding of bonsai shaping, i.e. using different methods to show that each plant and each variety has its own particular beauty. Right up to the present day the old traditional animal styles have retained their popularity in Chinese bonsai styling, and the Chinese love as much as ever root shapes bearing an uncanny resemblance to animals; also they like shapes having a symbolic meaning.

Also worth mentioning are the miniature landscapes so popular in China, arranged with stones, trees and figures, creating with some accuracy actual landscapes; they are, however, often made up only with stones. They are built up on flat trays or slabs arranged with water or white sand and so are really quite distinct from the Japanese *saikei*.

HOW TO GROW A BONSAI TREE

A general word about bonsai growing

ALMOST ALL trees and bushes growing in our latitudes are suitable as bonsai. The ideal varieties are those having a compact growth and developing small leaves.

To start growing a bonsai, that is to say, to grow a bonsai from suitable 'raw materials', the usual methods of plant propagation are used. Bonsai can be raised from seeds or cuttings bought from a nursery or collected from the wild.

Bonsai from seed

The secret here is to start small. Growing bonsai from seed is a hobby for people with a lot of patience. This is because it takes from between 5 to 7 years to grow a bonsai to style. However, it is possible to grow some very beautiful bonsai from seed as the development of the tree can be controlled right from the outset.

Although almost all plants can be raised as seedlings, there are varieties that are more suitable than others. Amongst the most popular are the conifers: Japanese cedar, larch, Japanese white, and black, pines. Amongst deciduous trees are all varieties of maple, birch, firethorn, ginkgo, pomegranate, hornbeam, cut-leafed beech and the zelkova (*Zelkova serrata*).

The most straightforward way of obtaining seed is either to collect it from the wild in autumn or to buy pre-packeted 'bonsai seed'. Whether your little trees will turn out just like the beautiful photographs on the seed packet rather depends on how well you grow them.

Prospective bonsai can be sown directly into compost, but they must have a frost-free environment. Seeds with hard husks germinate with more certainty and also quicker if the outside skin is first left to swell by soaking for a couple of days in water. Seed likely to germinate is heavy and will sink to the bottom;

Sorting the seeds
a) water
b) seeds able to germinate
c) unproductive seeds (floating)

Sowing
Above
a) seeds
b) fine compost
c) coarse gravel
   for drainage

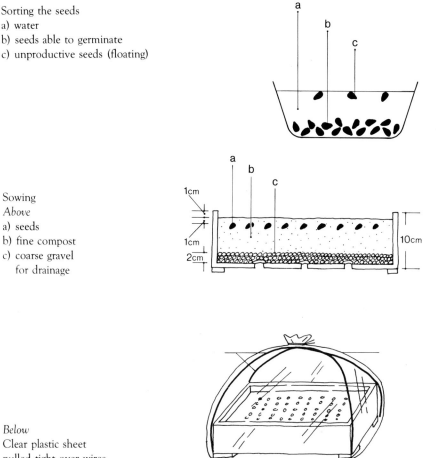

Below
Clear plastic sheet
pulled tight over wires

infertile seeds will float to the surface and can be discarded. Now comes the test of patience, especially as conifers need at least two to four months to germinate. On the other hand, deciduous trees push their way through in the first two months.

For sowing, a clay, ceramic, wooden or plastic container about 10 cm high is required. Pour 2 cm of grit for drainage into it. Next, fill the bowl up to 2 cm below the rim with a compost made from 1 part peat and 1 part sand. Lay out the seed carefully or, if it is particularly fine, scatter it gently direct from the seed packet and cover it with sand or compost. The covering layer of compost ½ – 1 cm thick is gently pressed down with a piece of wood. The seeds should then be watered with a can fitted with a very fine rose so that the compost is not washed away. Finally, the bowl should be covered with a sheet of glass or polythene and placed in a sheltered spot away from draughts and kept constantly damp.

When the first shoots break through the surface they will need air. Now a piece of wood should be wedged between the glass and the container. As soon as the first leaves develop remove the glass altogether and a dose of liquid manure should be applied at about half the recommended strength. Shaping can begin when the seedlings are 15–20 cm high.

Bonsai from cuttings

Growing from cuttings demands much less patience than germinating seeds. Almost all plants are suitable for this method: amongst conifers are Japanese cedar, cypress trees, yews, firs, juniper; amongst deciduous trees are azalea, maple, dwarf medlar, pomegranate, jasmine, olive, quince, willow, elm, rhododendron.

Another advantage of growing from cuttings has to do with the formation of the roots, as cuttings form a root-ball right from the start, whereas seedlings develop a taproot which has to be cut away.

Suitable material from deciduous trees and shrubs can be cut in the spring from new growth; cuttings from evergreens are taken later after the maturing of the new branches – from July to September.

Using a sharp knife, cut a shoot about 8–10 cm long from healthy parent stock and from underneath the base of a leaf.

Now the cutting, at this moment a rootless new shoot, must be prepared for its growth as an independent plant. First of all, remove all the leaves in that part of the stem that is to be

Cuttings are always cut at an
angle (top left)

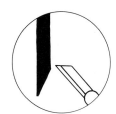

The centre drawing shows how
a number of cuttings can be
taken from one small branch. To
avoid rot the lower leaves
should be removed

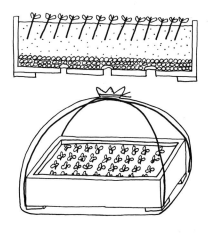

The cuttings are stuck into a
prepared plant container and
covered with polythene

stuck into the compost. Now stick the prepared young shoot into the same compost mixture as for the seedlings. More than one cutting can be planted in the same pot, but the leaves of the individual cuttings must not touch each other. In order to speed up the root growth, the cuttings can be dipped in hormone rooting powder or a rooting gel.

The bowl is then placed in a shady spot away from the wind and watered several times a day during the first few weeks. By 8 months at the latest, all the cuttings should have grown roots (the zelkova probably will have grown them by 4 weeks, but the juniper will have taken 6 to 8 months). Only then can the little plants be fed and accustomed to the sun.

In order to achieve a strong root system, cover the cuttings with polythene. In this way a greater humidity is achieved and the leaves will not wilt so quickly.

With the dwarf medlar, the willow and zelkova, for example, a good root system can be achieved by putting the cuttings in water, as is done for indoor plants. When sufficient roots have formed the cutting can be potted.

Bonsai from air-layering

Air-layering is the slow severing of a branch from the mother tree. By air-layering, new plants can be created from particularly beautiful branches and can be already trained to some extent whilst still attached to the mother plant. For the branch to be able to form roots easily, it should not be thicker than 3–5 cm. Especially suitable for air-layering are all varieties of maple, azalea, beech, Japanese cedar, fir, forsythia, firethorn, pomegranate, quince, rhododendron, elm, juniper, willow and zelkova.

In April, cut the branch with a tongue-cut, treat it with hormone rooting powder and wedge into the split a little moss or a small stone so that the tongue cannot grow together again.

Japanese black pine – informal upright, about 80 years old

Then wrap some damp sphagnum moss or peat inside polythene around the spot, close it up, and make it airtight with adhesive tape. Depending on the variety, roots will appear from 6 weeks, and as late as 12 to 24 months. Particularly quick to develop roots are willow and privet (in about 6 weeks), while rhododendrons and beech need twice as long; conifers need 12 to 24 months. When roots have developed, the young plants can be cut completely away and potted. Right from the start they can be cared for just like any other bonsai. Another method of air-layering is shown in the drawing below:

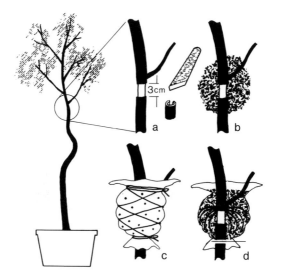

Here a bonsai with an ugly trunk is to be air-layered:
a) A ring of bark is removed with a knife
b) The part that has been cut away is now covered with moss
c) and is wrapped around with perforated polythene – a little less tight at the top end than the bottom in order to facilitate watering
d) As soon as sufficient roots have formed the branch is separated and planted in a bonsai pot

Bonsai propagation by layering

The layering method is the most suitable one for bushes and trees with low hanging branches, such as magnolias, forsythia, pines and weigela.

In order to layer a branch, bend it downwards and remove all the leaves and needles where the branch is to enter the ground. Then make a long cut about 4 cm long on the underside of the branch in order to assist the growth of roots. The branch prepared in this way should then be buried 10 cm deep in the ground and kept evenly damp at this point. Only when sufficient roots have formed can the branch then be severed from the mother plant.

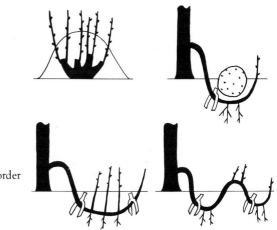

Different ways of layering in order to obtain young plants

Gathering wildlings

However attractive it may seem, simply to gather nicely grown and unique little trees and shrubs on the next spring walk in the woods, on a mountain or beside a lake, in order to save years of work and patience in sowing and air-layering, can bring one into conflict with the law in many countries and consequently a lot of trouble along with it. It is therefore absolutely necessary to obtain permission beforehand from the forestry authorities or private owner on discovering a particularly well shaped 'bonsai' that you would like to dig up. After obtaining permission, the plant should be removed with as much earth and as many roots as possible.

Then the new acquisition is planted in the garden or in a large container. After one or two years it can be put in a smaller pot and trained further.

Bonsai by grafting

Grafting is widely used in bonsai growing. With cuttings, for example, a part of the plant is simply pushed into the ground in such a way as to make root growth possible.

Propagation by grafting requires a nicely grown trunk to serve as 'rootstock' and a 'scion', a branch usually of the same variety. These two parts of the plant are then bound together in such a way so that they grow together and form a unit capable of surviving. By this somewhat difficult method the time required to grow bonsai can be reduced considerably. In this way not only can trees be propagated but also, by grafting on one or more branches, even shaping mistakes can be corrected and the overall shape of the bonsai improved. Usually the tree used as rootstock is of the same variety as the scion, but very often very different plant characteristics can be combined by grafting.

An example of this is the grafting in of a scion of the slow-growing Japanese white pine onto the quick-growing, long-needled Japanese black pine. The result of this grafting is a short-needled, quick-growing white pine – a much sought after type of bonsai.

Another example of grafting is to use a sparsely blossoming variety of wild apricot as rootstock with the branch

Beech – multiple trunk
The white bark is particularly charming in this variety of beech

of a full-blossoming, grafted apricot. In the region of the trunk and branches the new plant takes on the characteristics of the scion, whereas the stock will determine the roots and possibly the lower part of the trunk, just depending on whereabouts the graft has been made. Grafting demands some skill and experience in order to avoid unsightly swellings at the point of grafting, but the advantages outweigh the drawbacks:

- A new plant obtained by grafting blossoms and starts bearing fruit much more quickly than those not grafted. When, for example, branches that blossom and bear fruit are grafted onto a trunk that has not yet blossomed, the newly created tree will blossom and fruit as a seedling.

- Through grafting, a swifter development of trunk growth is obtained than by propagation with cuttings – the tree grows to the required trunk diameter much faster.

- As has already been mentioned, some of the methods of grafting are valuable ways of correcting bonsai shapes.

When is the time to graft?

The right time for grafting is just after the end of the tree's period of dormancy and just before it begins to sprout, that is, at the beginning of spring. Evergreen trees can be grafted not only from the middle of February until the middle of March but also from about the middle of August until the middle of September.

Types of graft

Amongst the different methods of grafting the following are of most interest to bonsai enthusiasts:

- Tip grafting
- Side grafting
- Budding
- Branch grafting (air inarching)

A rootstock of about 20 cm in length is the most suitable for *tip grafting (split grafting)* and *side grafting*. The best place to cut is as low down on the trunk and as near the roots as possible, so that the point of grafting is less obvious or can be covered with soil.

The rootstock is cut with a vertical incision exactly in the centre and the prepared scion set into it. To make a scion, a branch is cut about 5 cm long and the end trimmed to a wedge shape. If the scion is as thick as the rootstock it can be inserted into the vertical incision in the middle of the stock described above.

If the scion is much thinner than the stock, then it is set into the side. This method is known as a *side graft*.

To propagate a new tree, an incision is made into the

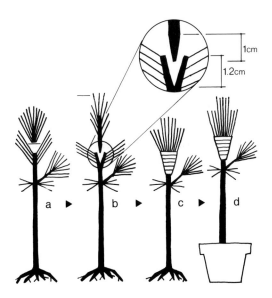

Example of tip grafting on a black pine:
a) Cut a split into the rootstock
b) Insert a scion cut to a wedge-shape into the split
c) Hold firm with raffia or a rubber band
d) Pot and water well

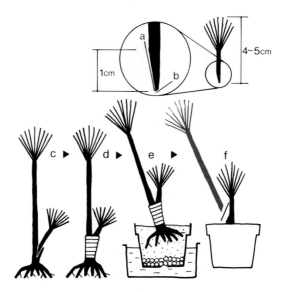

Example of side graft on a black pine:
a) Cut the scion at an angle
b) Cut off the tip of the cut from the other direction
c) Insert the scion in the stock
d) Close the point of grafting with raffia or a rubber band and seal with tree wax
e) Plant the tree in a pot with the scion upright. Lower the whole pot carefully into water, but do not let the fresh graft get wet!
f) Whether the scion has taken or not will be clear in the next year when the fresh shoots appear. It is only then that the upper part of the rootstock can be cut away

side of the rootstock, again as near as possible to the roots, but this time at that point on the trunk where a new branch is to be inserted.

The 5 cm long scion is cut diagonally across the end and inserted deep into the slit. Make sure that the diagonal and shorter side of the scion is put against the trunk of the rootstock, then the new branch, the scion, will grow out of the trunk at a natural angle.

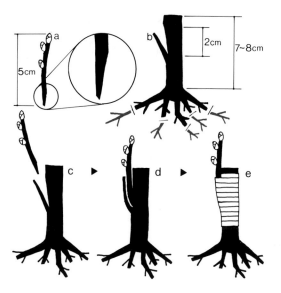

Method of grafting by side grafts on a Japanese apricot:

a and b)   A branch from the previous year's growth with 3–4 buds about 5 cm long is used as a scion. The rootstock is a 3–4 year old wild apricot grown from seed

c, d and e) Bring the cambium of the rootstock and the scion together, then prune the roots of the stock

Should a branch be required to complete the shape of the tree, a scion of the same variety can be taken and grafted into the desired place

After inserting the scion into the rootstock, bind up the whole with raffia. The graft point should then be sealed with tree wax.

If the scion begins to sprout the next year, then it has taken. The raffia can then be removed, the top of the rootstock is cut off above the graft point and again sealed with wax. There is now a new little tree.

If, when using the side-grafting method only, one tree is being grown, the raffia should be left on for a year as a support for the graft whilst it is growing.

With budding, instead of using a scion, a little piece of bark with a well-formed eye (branch bud) is set into the rootstock. In the following year this bud will grow into a branch.

The bark of the plant to be budded is cut with a sharp knife in a T-shape. First a 2 cm long vertical cut is made down to the wood, and then above this a further cut is made across to the same depth. Now the eye to be set into the stock is prepared and taken from a shoot that has matured to wood, the bud scion. The piece of bark around the eye should have a diameter of around 1 cm. The bark of the T-piece is lifted carefully with a budding knife, the flaps of bark are opened and the eye slipped in from above, and finally the bark on either side of the eye is pressed down tightly. The budding point is then bound tightly with raffia. Care must be taken to see that the eye remains free so that it can sprout next year.

The best time for budding is in July, when the plants are full of sap, as at this time the bark comes off easily from the trunk. To ensure that the budding point does not dry out, it is essential that the work be done on a cool day and as quickly as possible.

Branch grafting or air inarching is often a graft from the same tree, i.e. rootstock and scion come from the same mother plant. Using this method, a long branch can be grafted onto the same bonsai and multiple trunks formed by tying down a branch seated low down and joining it to the trunk. Also, missing branches can be set into the trunk.

In contrast to the other grafting methods, the scion is not immediately cut off. This is done when it has grown firmly onto the stock.

First of all, at the point where scion and rootstock are to grow together the bark is removed – a strip of bark around 3 cm long is removed from both. The cut surfaces are then placed together, bound tightly with raffia and then sealed with wax. Scion and rootstock will have grown together by late autumn of the same year if the work was undertaken at the beginning of spring, but conifers can take up to a year. Not until then can the scion be separated from the mother plant and then as low down on the trunk as possible in order to keep the bulge at the graft as small as possible.

The tree can be prepared for this operation by letting a branch grow near to the 'missing' one, and then later on it can be bent down to a graft at the point desired.

The illustration on p48 includes a working diagram showing how to graft the branches of different bonsai (of the same variety, of course). The plants are put close to each other in order to facilitate the binding together at the required point.

Care of the plants after grafting

After grafting, all plants are pruned severely, watered well, put in a position protected from the wind, and kept at an even temperature. A cold frame or polythene tunnel is recommended.

After the scion has sprouted – the sign that the graft has been successful – the plant is ready to be acclimatised to normal environmental conditions. At this time careful feeding can begin.

The following bonsai varieties are suitable for grafting:

Maple, apricot, peach, Japanese quince, crab apple, pomegranate, ginkgo (from the deciduous trees); and the Japanese white, and black, firs and juniper (from the conifers).

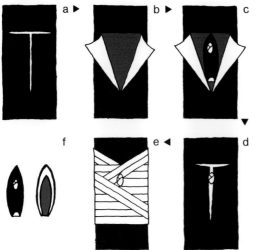

Budding:
a) Make a T-cut
b) Expose the cambium layer
c) Insert the bud
d) Join the scion together again
e) Bind tightly with raffia or a rubber band, but the eye must remain exposed
f) Front and back view of a bud scion

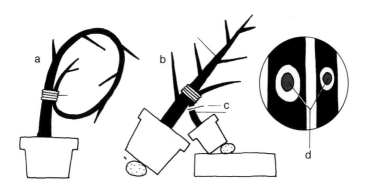

Branch grafting:
a) Place the cambium layer of the two plant sections together and bind them tightly
b) Bind the rootstock and the scion together
c) After they have grown together cut them apart
d) In order to enable them to grow together the cambium layers of the stock and scion must be joined together

Red maple – multiple trunk

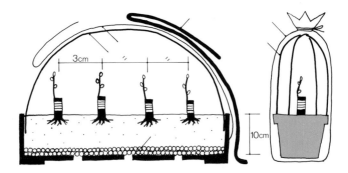

Freshly grafted plants should be well watered. A little 'greenhouse' should be built. Wires or bamboo canes are bent to make a framework for the cover and stuck into the corners. A perforated polythene sheet is stretched over the framework. After about a month the grafts will begin to sprout. At night, straw matting is placed over the polythene to keep the temperature even

Bonsai from nursery trees

If you are not keen to grow from seed or to take cuttings, and have no opportunity to collect from the wild, and it is healthy, strong plants from the specialist that you want, here is where the tree nurseryman can help. Here you are able to choose a plant for training as a bonsai. A tree purchased in this way has an advantage in that directly the roots have been pruned they can be potted in a bonsai container.

Ideally buy at the usual planting times: spring and autumn. Roots and branches can be pruned immediately. A training technique such as wiring weakens the plant and therefore can only be undertaken after the roots have re-established themselves and the plant has got used to its environment.

From the young plant a bonsai is created

When plants grown from seeds, or cuttings, have reached a height of 15–20 cm, the training and shaping of the prospective bonsai can begin. In order to control the height of the tree the roots must be pruned; the desired shape is achieved by trimming and wiring.

First the roots are cut back by a third. When planting the tree in a container or flower pot, arrange the roots so that they radiate from the trunk, making sure that primary roots do not cross over each other.

Some trees such as the pine and the juniper grow taproots. The taproot interferes with the arrangement of the roots and should be removed.

Every one to two years the growing trees will need fresh compost.

The first time the tree is repotted, compost consisting of one part peat and one part coarse sand should be used. A freshly repotted plant should be put in a shady corner away from the wind and only carefully introduced to the sun. Only after six weeks can it be given any liquid feed.

Before the first pruning can take place and the first wires be introduced, the tree must reach a certain age. In its second year the branches can be pruned for the first time. The trunk and main branches can be wired after 3 to 4 years – often essential with conifers. After 5 to 6 years the tree can be planted in a bonsai bowl.

As with repotting, spring is the best time for pruning. First, remove all buds and shoots growing in an undesirable direction (see the section on pruning the branches, pp55ff). As with miniature bonsai the weak branches can be encouraged by removing the strong ones. If the main shoot, that is to say the tip of the tree, is removed, the side shoots will grow more strongly. If the side shoots grow strong, they have to be evenly supported. In training a deciduous bonsai, regular pruning is often sufficient and wires are unnecessary. Deciduous trees make life easy for the careful observer: every bud reveals, by the direction in which it is pointing, how future branches will develop if the branch above the bud is cut away.

TRAINING A BONSAI

Some general remarks

A SUCCESSFUL BONSAI will look effectively like the larger tree in the wild, stylised, perhaps a little too perfect, but natural all the same; above all, it will be healthy. Until now the training of bonsai has followed Japanese examples, but without doubt they can be modelled on European trees. Perhaps European bonsai enthusiasts will soon be developing their own styles.

Many bonsai growers collect photographs of trees and woodlands or sketch them in the wild in order to use them as a pattern. Also bonsai books, exhibitions and courses provide stimulus for styles. Important for good shaping is a schooled eye able to discern clear lines and focal points in a tree, all to be underlined and developed in the shape.

An important feature is size; in order to achieve this miniature growth the plant pot must not be too big. The plant should not be allowed to develop too many roots and to take too much food. In addition, branches, twigs and roots must be regularly pruned and the shoots and buds pinched out. The trees should look like healthy miniature plants which, through the influence of their environment, perhaps in the mountains or because of poor soil, have remained small.

Without any intervention, the best bonsai loses its original created shape and proportions. The strong branches become even stronger and the weaker ones die away. As with all other kinds of trees, the main points of growth are at the tip of each branch. The further down the tree the branches are to be found the weaker will be their growth. The vertical growing trunk has the greatest strength; it can absorb the most food

A 25-year-old zelkova in full leaf

above the roots. Irregular branches spoil the shape of the bonsai. For this reason the new shoots should be removed in good time from the strongly growing branches, or alternatively branches can be bent downwards. This is also a way of holding back the growth.

The aim of bonsai training is to draw up the tree into the desired shape and to keep it in this shape. In this respect attention should be paid to the following points.

The bonsai container should be chosen with great care, the amount of compost must be carefully measured, and right from the beginning there should be a clear idea of the size and proportions of the bonsai in its final form.

The desired branches are kept and everything unnecessary pruned away.

The new shoots must be removed in good time.

By means of wiring, branches growing too close together can be held apart, so that the wind and the sun reach all leaves to the same extent.

Plucking off or cutting new shoots

Shortening and plucking off new shoots is one of the most important elements of bonsai training. This intervention in the growth of the tree serves not only to preserve the shape and size of a plant, but causes the growth usually concentrated at the tips to move down to branches in the lower reaches. The lower branches will then begin to grow strongly and the normally long growing period of the tree will be reduced.

The more often the new shoots of a tree are cut back the more compact and full of twigs the crown of the tree will be. How often this needs to be done depends largely on the species of tree. Zelkovas and maples belong to those trees which are cut back during the whole growing period, spring to autumn. Others, such as the Japanese white pine and beeches, are cut back only once a year, the best time being from the end of March to the beginning of April, whilst the new shoots are still soft.

Leaf cutting

In the case of many deciduous trees, leaves, branches and the trunk are disproportionate; the leaves are usually too large and detract from the overall effect of the tree.

By cutting the leaves at the right time, the tree can be made to produce tiny leaves.

In this process, using a leaf cutter or a pair of sharp scissors, the first leaves are completely removed, but not until they are fully grown. In our climatic zone this is in June/July. Almost all deciduous trees are able to renew their leaves; they go through a feigned autumn and then develop leaves that are smaller than the ones previously removed; also the tips of the branches become finer and more compact, and the autumnal colouring of the tree becomes considerably more beautiful. This radical process can only be undertaken on a strong and healthy bonsai.

Leaf cutting can affect the strength of whole branches. If the branch needs to become stronger, then it must be allowed to retain its original leaves, only the other, stronger branches having their leaves removed. A branch dominating the whole appearance of the tree too much will have its leaves removed, whilst branches around it retain theirs.

In order to protect a bonsai tree, it is preferable not to remove all its leaves at one time, but just half at first, and the rest after two weeks. The leaf stalk should, whenever possible, be left on the branch. Only on trees having very short stalks is this not possible, as for example on zelkovas. Here the leaves have to be removed in their entirety. After cutting off the leaves the tree does not need much water.

Cutting off branches

The removal of branches establishes the basic shape of the tree. It is therefore necessary to know from the start how the tree is going to look later, and to take into account which shape best suits the particular tree.

Branches directly opposite each other or directly above each other, as well as those growing out towards the viewing side, along with those growing at the same height are all removed; also side branches that disturb the whole effect of the bonsai by their direction of growth should be cut away.

Special cutters that make a concave cut are used to remove branches. In this way the place where the branch was cut away heals more quickly, with only a tiny scar remaining.

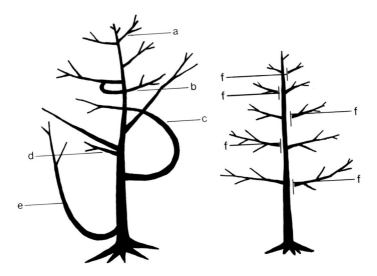

a) One branch of any two growing at the same height on the trunk is removed
b) Branches growing forward across the trunk are also removed
c) Branches growing in a U-shape are removed
d) Any branch growing too close above another must be removed
e) The bottom third of the trunk should remain free of branches
f) Right and left of the trunk branches growing opposite each other should be removed alternately

An apple tree in full blossom

Thickening the trunk and branches

A dense crown and a thin trunk are disproportionate and therefore disturb the harmony. If the bonsai has grown in this way, the trunk needs thickening. This means that its growth must be stimulated so that it can gain in strength quickly. This is achieved by leaving the lower branches on the trunk until the required thickness is reached, as these branches determine the diameter of the trunk.

There is an alternative method of stimulating the growth of the trunk. In spring, a piece of aluminium wire is tied around the base of the trunk, just above the soil. During the summer, the trunk above the wire will swell considerably. You must not forget to remove the wire again in the autumn, to prevent the bonsai dying.

Thin branches can be thickened too, by leaving on all shoots and leaves; the more leaves a branch has to carry the stronger it becomes, because the nutrient exchange increases – and whoever eats more, increases in size! When the branch has reached the required size, the wild growth disturbing the optical harmony can be cut away.

Training individual varieties of bonsai

Conifers

The way to remove new shoots of conifers, such as Japanese black pine and white pine, is shown on the diagram on p64, centre.

In the case of the needle juniper and the Japanese cedar, new shoots are nipped out, using the fingers, just as they open, throughout the whole growing period. On branches having few new shoots, or showing weak growth, and on branches that are to grow further, only a few new shoots should be pinched out.

Deciduous trees

Maple, beech and zelkova should wherever possible possess fine twigs and have small leaves. New shoots on these trees need to be continually pinched out before they grow too large.

On pomegranate trees and the hornbeam, new shoots are shortened as soon as they have grown to around 5-7 cm. They are then cut back to one or two leaves from the base of the shoot.

Flowering and fruiting trees

On Japanese apricots, Japanese quince, crab apple and azaleas, the new shoots must be left to open out. At the beginning of June to the middle of July they are then cut back.

Pratical advice on the training
of the most important bonsai plants

Maple (Acer) varieties

The new shoots of the maple are pinched out back to two eyes, i.e. two pairs of leaves. As the shoots develop differently, this work tends to be spread over the whole of the growing season. Older plants grow very much more slowly. For this reason it is better to cut them back only in spring, and, even then, very early in order to avoid a long wait between the leaves. When cutting the leaves, leaf stalks should be left on the branches, as this protects the plant.

Firs (Abies and Picea)

New shoots, that have grown to 2-3 cm in length, and which will still be soft, should be pinched out with the fingertips with a light twisting movement to a third of their length. This work takes three to four weeks as the longest shoots are pinched out first (2–3 cm) and then the others when they have developed this length.

Chinese Juniper (Juniperus chinensis)

The new shoots are pinched out with the fingertips during the whole of the growing period to a fan shape, so that the juniper gets an even, fresh green cushion.

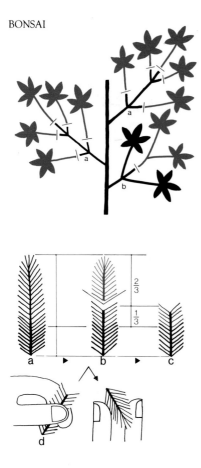

Pinching out new shoots and cutting
the leaves on maple
a) Cutting the leaves: each time leave
   a short piece on the stalk
b) Pinch back new shoots to one pair
   of leaves

Pinching out new shoots on firs
a) New shoots and those from the
   previous year
b) Pinch back the shoot by a third
c) Hold the base of the shoot firmly
   when pinching out

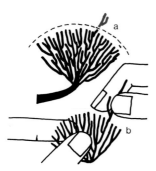

Pinching out new shoots on Chinese
juniper
a) Pinch out the fine shoots in such a
   way as to form a gentle curve
b) Hold firmly with one hand and
   pinch out up to the remaining
   length

Pinching out wilted blossom and cutting the branches on Japanese apricots
a) Cut back up to 1–2 joints on the branch
b) Remove wilted blossoms

Cutting back shoots that have grown too long on Japanese apricots

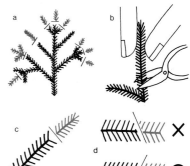

Cutting new shoots on Japanese cedar a), b) and c)
Cut back shoots that have grown too long with scissors
d) Do not cut across the needles, otherwise brown scars will occur

Japanese apricot (Prunus mume)

When blossomtime is over, all the previous year's shoots are cut back to one or two leaf joints. Any remaining faded blossoms must be removed, because if they have been fertilised they would bear fruit otherwise. On an apricot tree, in constrast to apple trees, the fruit is undesirable as it does not look particularly pretty and only serves to weaken the tree unnecessarily. On these trees it is the magnificence of the blossom that is most prized. At the end of September the tips of the current year's shoots are cut back, leaving four or five leaf joints. Shoots that have not developed more than four or five leaf joints should not be cut back. This is to ensure that the growing strength is evenly divided in all branches of the trees so that the blossom will then be evenly distributed all over it. Apricots are repotted in spring immediately after blossoming, as in the case of all bonsai blossoming before sprouting leaves. This is because, otherwise, the root pruning taking place at the same time would seriously endanger the ripening of the blossom.

Japanese cedar (Cryptomeria japonica)

From the beginning of July onwards gradually pinch out the new shoots so that the needle tips grow evenly. At the same time, it is recommended that branches too close together are cut away along with any extraneous branches. Both operations assist correction to the shape of the bonsai.

Cut-leaved beech (Fagus sylvatica var.)

The growth of the cut-leaved beech is concentrated particularly in the upper branches, whereas the branches below do not grow so well and are weaker. The cut-leaved beech is a type of bonsai in which the proportions of the tree are not easy to maintain. Begin to pinch out when the new leaf buds just begin to develop shoots in spring. With the fingertips, the leaf buds are pinched out to just two eyes. Where strong growth is being encouraged, pinching out can be undertaken at a later date. In this case the new shoots are pinched out when they have reached the point where growth has come to a standstill. They are then cut back to three or four leaf shoots. In the case of very young bonsai, one should wait until all new shoots are fully grown before pinching out or cutting. The time lapse for pinching out between the strong and the weak shoots should be about two to three days.

Japanese white pine *(Pinus parviflora)*

Around May, the Japanese white pine has strong new shoots. These shoots must be first nipped out of the crown of the tree and then everywhere where new shoots show particularly strong growth. Using these measures, the irregular growth of the new shoots can be corrected. Where lots of shoots grow out at the same time, the strongest candle – this is what shoots are called on pines – must be broken out completely. In the case of a single shoot that has grown quite strongly, a third of the shoot should be left. As a rule new shoots on Japanese white pine should be pinched out to two or three needle rings.

Zelkova *(Zelkova serrata)*

In just the same way as other deciduous trees, new shoots on the zelkova appear in spring and they must be pinched out right away. If the branches are to be refined, then all new shoots should be pinched out again and again. It is the refined branches of the zelkova that appeal so much to bonsai growers.

Shoots are easier than most to pinch out as long as they are still soft. For this reason, they are always pinched back to one or two buds. First of all the strongest, then the not so strong, and then the weak shoots are all pinched out.

This method leads to an even growth of the bonsai. Holding back the concentrated growth of the shoots in this way causes shorter growth between branch joints and leads to the development of finer branches and smaller leaves, so that the bonsai in the end attains the desired shape.

Pinching out new shoots on cut-leaved beech
a) On younger plants shorten to 3-4 leaf shoots
b) With older plants new shoots that are just breaking through should be pinched out with the fingers

Pinching out new shoots on Japanese white pine
a) Cut back strong shoots to the length of shorter shoots
b) Take out the stronger shoots from the base

Pinching out new shoots and cutting the leaves on zelkova
a) Pinch out the shoot eyes with the fingertips
b) Cut or pinch out the leaves

Pinching out is always undertaken during a period of about six months when new buds have developed, that is to say, just after the tree begins sprouting until autumn when the tree ends its growing time.

On shoots that grow too strongly, here too the leaves are cut away in order to reduce growth. Cutting the leaves enables the growth of the branches to be evened out while also producing a multiplicity of fine branches and small leaves. In this way the bonsai obtains a better formed network of branches than is often the case with older trees, and it looks even more beautiful as a result. When cutting the leaves of a zelkova, it is possible to reach the inner recesses of the branches without causing any damage by using long narrow bonsai scissors. The outer leaves can be removed later with the fingers.

Pinching out and shortening needles
of the Japanese black pine

The cutting of the needle shoots on Japanese black pines (Pinus thunbergii) is carried out in order to reduce the number of needles. The beautiful appearance of the short fresh needles is something especially valued by bonsai enthusiasts. Pruning takes place from the middle of June until the beginning of July, when the new shoots are growing strongly and have completely opened. During this period, the growth of the new shoots is uneven, even after having been pinched out in spring. So now a beginning is made on the lower branches, those weak branches growing close to the trunk. In gaps of around seven to ten days the rest of the shoots are cut away. By using this method an even length of all shoots is achieved.

Because the needles grow closely and thickly the bonsai does not obtain an even ventilation. Also, light does not reach all branches. All the new shoots would grow very poorly and wither, if a section of the old needles is not pinched out to bring light into the tree. This work is undertaken between May and August.

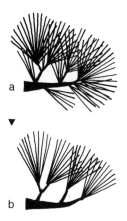
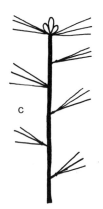

Pinching out the needles on Japanese black pines a) and b):
Pinch out older and dry needles harmed by drought and sunshine

c) After pinching out the needles immediately on the new shoots, leaving about 6 pairs of needles, on the rest leave 3 pairs of needles

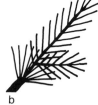
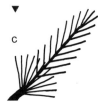

Cutting the needle shoots on black pines
a) Always remove each of the shortest shoots
b) in gaps of around 7–10 days
c) The first shoot is taken off
d) The second shoot is taken off
e) All new shoots are now removed
f) A new, compact mantle of needles forms

The reason for, and the technique of wiring

Wiring is a means of training bonsai. For periods of several months wires are wrapped around the trunk and branches in order to induce them to adopt a new position. By wiring, the tree becomes pliant and only then is it possible to correct or reshape it. In order to master this technique, some skill and practice is required. This method makes possible an emphasis of the basic structure of the tree and its natural beauty, underlining its special attraction and character. Wiring is an artificial means by which within a relatively short space of time the planned shape can be achieved, and then the wires are removed.

Wiring the branches of deciduous trees, for example, enables important changes of shape to be made within a month or two, and the thicker branches of conifers in about a year. This method is always very effective when a rapid change of shape is required. In this way the important and unimportant branches can receive their proper emphasis. Also, through this method branches whose direction of growth does not fit in with the overall shape can be made to harmonise. The wires allow better ventilation and penetration by sunlight, as does the cutting away of branches, so contributing to a healthy cultivation of the bonsai. At all costs, however, imposing a direction of growth by force is to be avoided. If the tree remains wired for too long or is bound too tightly, wiring loses its value. It has, in fact, exactly the opposite effect. Because wiring demands some practice it is recommended that beginners choose a bonsai already shaped and requiring no extreme changes. A small correction, for example, involving only a slight change of direction in the branches, is not difficult to effect.

Tools for wiring

Copper or aluminium wire:

Copper wire is soft and malleable, but despite this offers sufficient grip. Different thicknesses are used – for branches or trunk – as required. With deciduous trees, whose bark is very sensitive, such as maple, zelkova or Japanese apricot, generally aluminium wire is used in order to avoid damage to the bark.

Branch cutters:

Before wiring, the branches should already be pruned. A pair of branch cutters cut better than ordinary clippers as its concave cut leaves a slight hollow, enabling the bark to heal over quickly and cleanly.

Wire cutters, pliers:

In order to bend over the end of the wire, pliers are needed. A wire cutter is absolutely essential in order to remove wires from around the tree. The removal of the wires demands a steady hand so that no serious injuries occur to the bark.

When is wiring done?

Conifers are best wired between the end of October and the next spring, before the tree sends out its shoots. After sprouting, a tree should no longer be wired, as the young shoots could easily be damaged. Deciduous trees are wired when the tree carries no leaves, ideally before it throws out shoots in the spring. The wiring of zelkovas and maples is best undertaken when pruning, just before the shoots begin to grow. If new branches on deciduous trees need to be wired, this work is undertaken in May and June. As a rule, wiring should never be undertaken on freshly repotted bonsai, but postponed for at least a month. Wiring should neither be undertaken on hot days, when they are in any case weakened by heat, nor on frosty winter days, as in the greater cold the branches are stiff and break easily.

Wiring can be used as a way of correcting the shape of trunks and branches that have lost their optical balance. In order to correct the shape of the bonsai more rapidly one cannot simply bend a branch by force into an empty space just to give the impression of better proportion. It is possible to deal

a) The end of the wire should
   be stuck into the compost
   from behind the tree
   diagonally to the bottom of
   the container
b) Do not bind too tightly
c) Wind gently in an upward
   spiral
d) Bend the branch carefully

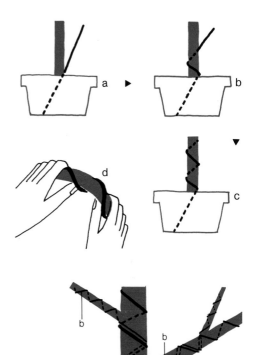

Basic rules of winding around trunk
and branch
a) The tree is wound around from the
   base of the trunk with wire –
   branches with a suitable thinner
   one
b) The gaps between the windings of
   wire should be the same distance
   apart

Through wiring the branch is to be
trained somewhat upwards, as here
with a Japanese white pine

with this in other ways. Before wiring, the bonsai must be carefully studied from all sides in order to establish which branches are to be retained and wired. Time must be taken to consider the appearance of the tree and to imagine how it will eventually look when the undesirable branches are cut away. It is not the technique of cutting in itself, but the ability to sense the future shape of the bonsai and a feeling for space and proportion that is crucial.

Before wiring one should try to bend branches in the desired direction in order to test tension and resistance. Only then can the most suitable wires be readily chosen. Freshly repotted or older bonsai possessing brittle branches (e.g. azalea varieties) should be handled with great care.

How is wiring carried out?

The proper procedure when wiring is to work from the base of the trunk to the tip of the tree, from the lower to the upper branches, from the base of the branches to their tips. Wiring should be wound in a spiral, always in the direction of growth. The wire should, at the same time, be closely wound, but not too tightly. The end of the spiral of wire is held fast by a bend in the wire. The distance between the individual turns depends upon the extent to which the trunk or the branch is to be bent. If the distance between the turns is narrow, the effectiveness of the wire is reduced and bending becomes more difficult.

Caring for a wired plant

A bonsai that has just been wired must, as after every intervention, be allowed to recover. For the first two days without fail, it should be sprayed late in the afternoon.

This applies to Japanese cedar and needle junipers in particular. Because of the extra pruning of the branches required, these are often subjected to severe training and need plenty of time to recover. For this reason such bonsai should always be given a shady place. It is very easy when bending a branch for a split or crack to occur. When this happens the spot must be protected from air and water and the wounds immediately sealed with tree wax.

How long must the wire remain on the plant?

It is especially important that wires on deciduous trees and young conifers be removed at the proper time, before the bark begins to grow. Conifers remain wired for between one to one and a half years. The wire on deciduous trees on the other hand will sink very quickly into the bark. Wiring should therefore be kept from two to four months. If the desired shape is not quite achieved, it is recommended that the wiring be repeated.

One should not be impatient, if things do not work out completely first time round. A change of shape is achieved only bit by bit. With conifers it is not easy to effect desirable changes of shape by wiring, because the trunk is very hard and does not easily bend. For this reason wiring must often be repeated several times.

Example: wiring a Japanese white pine

First of all, remove all superfluous lower branches and twigs. The main line of the trunk and its main branches can then be seen more readily, so that the viewing side can be decided upon and the planned basic shape established.

The length of wire required for correcting the trunk should be one and a half times the height of the tree. Begin by burying the wire in the compost behind the trunk (see illustration p69 above).

The wire is then wound in a spiral up the trunk, ensuring that there is only light pressure on the bark. After the trunk, the most important branches are wired so that the basic shape of the tree is established. Wiring and bending is always done from the lower to the higher branches.

After wiring, the whole harmony of the bonsai will be looked at again.

Training a forest group

Mixed forests are especially attractive and gracious in winter, the delicate twigs of their trees open to the light. The forest group, called *Yose ue*, is an imitation of natural woodlands. Its beauty is quite different to that of a single bonsai, being expressed instead by the grouping of the trees. Coniferous woods establish the pattern for the forest group. The trunks of the pines stretch towards the heavens, their delicate and slender branches setting them apart from mixed forests. Patterns for the forest group are to be found in those little woods and groves found in country areas such as lakesides and on small islands.

Forest groups should ideally have at least three individual trees in them; some tree groups consist of very many, up to several dozen single trees. They are planted in flat trays according to the following basic principles.

At the centre of every forest group three trees dominate. First of all, a large attractive tree is selected as the primary tree, the second largest as a secondary tree and then the third largest. The other trees should be smaller and thinner than the three main trees. The total number of trees for a forest group, according to Japanese understanding, must always be an odd number, such as 5, 7, 9, etc., and by avoiding all evenness a natural effect is created. Depending on the number of trees, a suitable tray should be selected. Naturally the choice of tray is almost infinite, but in the end it is determined largely by the size and number of trees. However, harmony and balance in the overall design must not be overlooked.

A representation of perspective can be achieved through an arrangment of trees of different sizes so that the forest group then mirrors its larger pattern in nature.

This trident maple shows itself in all its beauty.
The flowering cushion of moss underlines the attractiveness of the autumn colours

Forest group of conifers

The material for forest groups can be gathered from young conifers, such as firs, pines and larches, all of which can be bought from a nursery. They will be about three to five years old and pot grown, but with roots still not yet strongly developed.

The most suitable time for planting is generally between the middle of March and the middle of April.

Forest group using deciduous trees

Deciduous trees grown from seeds or cuttings are generally the best. The proper time for the planting of cut-leaved beech, trident maple, zelkova, etc. lies between February and the end of March, but without fail before the trees start to sprout.

The necessary material

- Plants of different sizes
- A flat tray of large enough diameter to accommodate a forest group
- Tools: cutters, chopsticks, wires, tweezers
- Soil and compost

Arranging the group

- Most of the compost should be carefully removed from the roots in advance. Spread out the soil evenly on the flat tray, the drainage holes having been covered beforehand with plastic mesh. Then the plants are arranged on the tray. Next, stand the primary tree on the tray. It should generally be positioned at a point a third of the way or halfway across the tray.
- The second largest tree, the secondary tree, should be placed to its left or right, somewhat behind the main tree. Whereas the main and secondary tree are placed close to each other, the third tree should stand some little way apart from these two. Now the rest of the trees are planted around this central

group. It is also important that the arrangement is always planted in the form of an uneven triangle. As the work progresses the smaller trees are anchored to the main or secondary tree with thin wires or threads.

- The forest group is a re-creation of woods and forests stretching into the distance, into infinity. This is the impression that must be given on the tray. If an optical illusion of this stretching out into the distance is to be achieved on the limited area of a tray, then there is only one method: the most careful planning and positioning of the individual trees, taking account of the respective shapes and sizes. The plants are not arranged in the centre of the tray, but are set to the left or right. In this way the focal point is shifted and so a 'dying away' effect is created. The smaller trees should be so arranged that this spatial illusion of distance is enhanced. This can be achieved by putting the taller trees towards the front and the smaller trees further back.

  If the trunks jut out over the edge of the tray, the effect of distance is heightened.

- In order to preserve the variety and harmony of the presentation, as has already been said, one should use as material trees of different heights and having trunks of different diameter. Variety is introduced to a forest group by the way in which the individual trees are arranged. As has already been pointed out, trees should not be positioned in the centre of the tray. Also the distance between the trees must be carefully weighed up. The group should be considered from different vantage points so that the distances between the trees do not appear to be the same.

  All plants should be arranged in such a way that no tree obscures another, when viewed from the front, from behind or from the side. It is important that two elements on the tray are united, namely 'movement' and 'rest'.

Pages 76 and 77: deciduous holly *(Ilex verticillata)* – forest group

BONSAI

- When everything is in place, compost is pushed between the roots using the chopsticks to prevent the individual trees from falling over. Sometimes the roots will have grown together so thickly that it is not possible to push soil between them with the fingers. The covering of compost is heaped a little higher around where the larger trees are planted. In the rest of the tray the soil is spread somewhat thinner in order to retain the perspective.

- The surface of the soil cover is dampened using a spray. Working outwards from the base of the tree trunks, the forest group is covered with moss. It is necessary to apply a little pressure to ensure that the moss sticks. The covering of moss does not only have the purpose of enhancing the appearance,

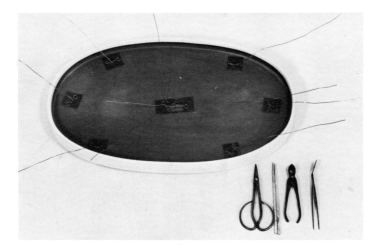

The drainage holes are covered with mesh. In order that the trees should not fall over whilst the arranging is going on, wires have been attached to the tray to which the trees can be secured. Below the tray (from left to right): pruning shears, chopsticks, branch cutters (concave cutters) and tweezers

it also prevents the surface of the soil drying out quickly and the compost from washing away when being watered.

Caring for a forest group

As when repotting, care should be taken to protect a freshly planted group from the wind, and to place it in a shady spot. Strong movements of air hinder root formation. Only after around 20 days can the forest group be brought out into the open. When watering, the leaves should be sprayed several times. The compost should not be too dry, but also not too wet. Around 20 to 30 days after planting a gentle feed can be given.

For the forest group a number of zelkova of different heights are brought together

The main tree is placed in position and made secure

Now the three trees forming the principal element of the forest group are arranged

The forest is completed

Last of all the smaller and thinner trees are arranged

A successful forest group

Rock-grown style

Rock-grown bonsai, called *ishitsuki*, are created by using small stones, miniature trees, grasses and moss to copy a rocky landscape. It is a very distinct style of presenting a natural landscape. The observer's unique impression of a section of a barren, unspoilt ravine, of a mountain landscape or seascape, is recreated on an island in a bonsai style. As a piece of rock or stone absorbs heat well and conserves it, the growth of bonsai on a rock will be stronger than in a pot, and can be trained in a much shorter period.

The rock is placed on a tray full of water or covered with sand. Water and sand symbolise the natural conditions at the seaside or in the mountain ravine. In valleys and gorges are to be found great varieties of rock that form a harmonious entity with the trees and grasses. Stone chosen for a rock-style bonsai should be carefully examined as to structure and grain.

Every stone has its own character. A rough, natural looking stone demands strong trees. For a stone showing a sweeping line, on the other hand, soft and gentle trees are more suitable. A stone with a more striking appearance calls for a tree with an interesting shape. The rock style is a very impressive style with which to represent a natural landscape.

There are two rock styles:

- There is the rock in a tray filled with water. In normal bonsai styles the tree is planted directly into the container. Instead of being planted in a pot, in this style trees are planted over a stone using a special compost.

- Another style involves planting the bonsai in a container with compost. The trees grow here in just the same way on a rock but the roots are fed from the soil in the tray.

Materials and tools

- Trees: almost all conifer and deciduous trees can be used for the rock style. Especially suitable are Chinese juniper, needle juniper, Japanese cedar, maple or zelkova.

- Stones: generally, all natural stones can be used, such as those found in ravines and mountains. Not suitable are those found on the beach as they hold too much salt. The stones should if possible be uneven or have a broken surface, as soil holds better on such stones. Also, these kinds of stone lend expression to the landscape.

- Compost: in order to enable trees and grasses to cling onto the sloping rocks, a soft compost is required that will give them a grip, 'keto-tsuchi', as the Japanese call it (a mixture of loam and peat in equal parts).

- Grasses as a 'supplement': wild grasses or dainty plants, such as dwarf azaleas, dwarf medlars and dwarf quinces, all smaller

Pages 84 and 85: rock style

than the main trees, can be arranged around the trees. This makes the rock-style arrangement more impressive. In this way the naturalness and character of the seasons can be better imitated.

- Other requirements: wires for securing the plants, quick-setting glue, cement powder, U-shaped pegs to secure the moss (these pegs can be made from wire).

The proper planting time

The best time to plant rock-style bonsai is in springtime, just at the beginning of the growing time, that is to say, just before they begin to sprout.

Firs, Japanese white and black pines, Chinese juniper, needle juniper and Japanese cedar are all best planted from March until the middle of April. Maple and zelkova are best planted from February until the end of March.

Arranging rock bonsai

- Before starting work, the compost is prepared and moss laid in water. The plants are taken out of their pots. The greater part of the soil around the roots must be carefully removed. In doing this, care must be taken to ensure that the roots are not torn off or cut in any way, even if they are too long.
- First it must be decided where the most suitable spot on the stone is for the plant to grow. When the stone and the plant are suitably matched, the wires to hold the plants secure are anchored by using a quick drying glue and cement powder.
- After watering the rock, the compost is spread on little by little where the plant is to be grown.
- Now the plant is positioned on the chosen place and the roots arranged around the rock. If there is not sufficient room, the roots can be arranged on top of one another. Then on top of the roots comes the compost.
- The wires are now fastened together and in this way the root system is secured to the rock. The wires remaining are trimmed back as necessary. Wires and roots are afterwards covered with compost.

- Wild grasses or small plants are added to them. These supplementary plants create the impression of a varied rock landscape. The roots are covered with compost and the plants secured.
- When the trees are all in place, once again as much compost as possible is poured around plants.
- The whole surface of the compost is covered with damp moss. On sloping or vertical surfaces moss can best be secured with U-shaped pegs of wire. They are stuck into the soil like hairgrips.
- After this the trees and moss are sprayed liberally with water.
- The planted rock is then placed on a tray full of water or compost.

A collection of materials for rock style: rocks with wires, glued together with an epoxy resin glue. Underneath (from left to right): azalea, euonymus and dwarf medlar as underplanting for the three firs. Underneath: branch cutters, shears, tweezers; alongside on the mesh, pieces of moss and compost formed into a ball

The main tree is set in place

The supplementary and third trees are planted

Constructing a rock-style
arrangement
a) Anchor wires at the point
   where the trees are to be
   placed
b) Smear it with the soil
   mixture
c) Position the trees and secure
   with wires
d) Put as much compost as
   possible over the wires and
   roots, then cover with moss.
   Using home-made U-shaped
   pegs hold the moss in place

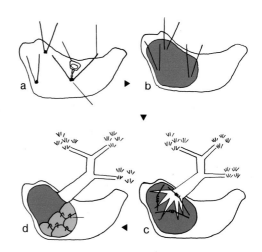

After positioning, the plants are secured with wire and covered with compost

Care of rock bonsai

As the roots cannot be pruned like other bonsai, the resistance of the root-ball is much weaker. A rock bonsai demands special care until the moss and the roots of the trees are properly grown.

Finished arrangement

Plant containers

Over the years the Japanese have developoed special bonsai containers and trays to suit the bonsai styles, and which do not distract from the tree, but harmonise plants and surroundings. In Europe, however, almost no special containers have been produced. 'True' bonsai containers available over here come largely from Japan and China.

A good bonsai has roots, a trunk, branches and leaves that are all in proportion with one another. The environment must suit the tree. The landscape in which it stands can be grown over with moss – and the landscape enclosed by the bowl. The buying of a container should be undertaken bearing in mind the following:

- Slanting bonsai styles, so-called cascades, should be planted in round or square containers, but upright styles in flat, rectangular or oval ones.
- Trees with close and heavy crowns need pots giving an impression of solidity.
- It is also important that the colours of the plants and the bowls harmonise. Flowering plants and those with bright green foliage, such as zelkova, are seen at their best in light, glazed pots. On the other hand, for trees with dark leaves the best choice is red, grey or brown plant pots.

Artificial ageing

The older a bonsai, the more strength of character it has and the more beautiful it is. Therefore, it has become popular to introduce artificial ageing. With these measures it is also possible to correct training errors.

Dead branches pointing to the heavens or shooting out strongly from the dark bark make a tree look older. It is a good idea to retain dead branches and give them special treatment. First remove the bark from the stump and sharpen it to a point, then paint it with a solution of lemon juice and considerably thinned furniture bleaching medium. This bleaches the branch and protects it from rot, and, because of its white appearance looks like ageing.

Bonsai that have shot up too high can be made to look shorter by removing the needles or leaves from the tips. Remove the bark from the tips of their branches and bleach them as outlined above.

Artificial ageing: a dead branch is not removed, but the bark is removed and bleached. The Japanese call this a *jin*

BUYING BONSAI

I N EUROPE, bonsai have become well known only
relatively recently, not really long enough for them to have
been bred here to any extent. For this reason most little
trees are imported from either Japan or China.

There is quite a large choice of young and old trees in
different varieties and styles.

A good bonsai has a clear, natural shape, and is strong and
healthy. It betrays through its leaves and growth the season at
the time.

A young bonsai with a harmonised shape can be more
valuable than an old and unpleasant example.

It is best to choose a tree from a specialist shop offering
after-sales care.

Marks of quality

A bonsai shows itself off – a beautiful one particularly!
When looking at a good bonsai it should be carefully
considered. Examine the trunk and note the arrangement of
the branches.

When looked at from above, the first thing to notice is that
a beautiful bonsai has only a few branches; secondly, no branch
hides another; and thirdly, no two branches are parallel or grow
at the same height. Ideally, the branches grow spirally around
the trunk, and no main branches grow towards the front,
towards the viewer.

The trees do not have so few branches naturally, especially
if they have been gathered from the wild or bought from a
nursery. If the branches have been professionally pruned, after a
few years the scars will grow so that they are virtually invisible.
Bad cuts reduce the value of a bonsai.

Much attention is paid to the shaping of branches during its
growth, because this determines the general character of the
bonsai. On a bent trunk the branches grow on the outer side of

Chinese juniper, about 800 years old

A colourful feather maple with a fascinating growth

the bend. Like the trunk, the branches should taper. Right up to the apex the tree becomes increasingly narrower.

A healthy tree gives the impression of being secure in the ground. The roots seen around the base of the trunk should be of differing diameters and not have a regular distance between them. It is most important, however, that any two roots do not cross over each other, but together form a good ring of roots.

It is not only the proportions between the root system, trunk and branches that give the bonsai a harmonious shape, but also the leaves. They should be as small as possible and have a healthy and strong colour to complete the picture.

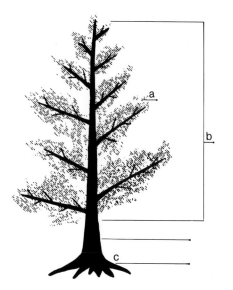

Quality characteristics of bonsai are:
a) the right proportions of the leaf to tree
b) the correct arrangement of the branches
c) the tapering of the trunk from the bottom to the top

HOW DO I LOOK AFTER MY BONSAI?

W HETHER YOU have grown your bonsai yourself or bought it, you will have become attached to it and wish to keep it healthy by proper care.

It is therefore necessary to repot at the correct time with the correct compost, to place it in a suitable location, and give it sufficient water and adequate feeding.

Certainly, now and again problems will arise for which this book will not provide adequate solutions – in which case you must refer to the specialist. Every good bonsai expert will be only too happy to advise you and to help your bonsai in his 'nursing ward', should it become sick or you go on holiday. Regular exchange of experience is to be had in bonsai clubs in many parts of the country.

Root pruning

A third or even a half of the roots can be cut away when repotting. This gives life to the roots. Besides this, sensible proportions remain between the continually pruned crown and root system.

Potting and repotting

Many tips about potting and repotting have been given in previous chapters. Actually, the bonsai is 'potted' only when it comes for the first time into a bonsai pot; later, one speaks of 'repotting'.

As soon as the compost is used up or the roots have to be supported, the bonsai needs repotting. Very old specimens are almost always planted back into the same container after renewing the compost. Only young trees require a 1–2 cm larger container every year or two. How quickly the compost becomes exhausted largely depends on the variety; quick growing deciduous trees need fresh compost every year or two, conifers every two to five years.

This is the way to repot correctly

Leave the bonsai before repotting to dry out a little so that the earth can be more easily removed. Lift the tree from the pot and carefully scrape away about half the soil from around the roots with chopsticks, working in from the edge. Then remove all damaged and dead roots, and cut away all around a third of the roots. In the case of thick roots, cut them so that the place cut faces downwards.

This is the way to prepare the pot

First of all the drainage holes are covered with a plastic mesh so that the earth cannot trickle away later on. Then, on the bottom of the tray, place a layer of rough gravel for drainage, no more than 2 cm deep, and on top of this a thin layer of bonsai soil. Next set out the plants with their root-ball in the pot and if necessary secure them to the base with aluminium or plastic-covered wire, for which purpose the wire is pulled through the drainage holes.

Now the hollows between the roots are filled with bonsai compost until it comes just under the rim of the bowl, and then it is pressed down with the thumbs. Remember that the fresh bonsai compost should be fairly dry so that it trickles more easily into the hollow spaces between the roots.

It has been already pointed out that the bonsai art largely consists of the way in which a bonsai is positioned in the

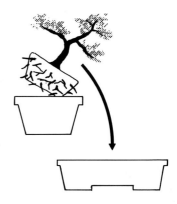

First find a suitable bowl

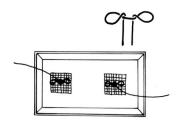

The plastic mesh over the drainage holes is secured to the bowl with the loop of wire (see above)

To secure the repotted tree, a wire is passed through the drainage holes

For drainage a layer of gravel is added

2cm

Using chopsticks, the compost is removed up to the main root-ball

After the soil is removed up to the main root-ball, the roots are cut back a third to half of their length

After setting the tree in position it is secured with wire but not exactly in the middle

Now fill up with compost

Using chopsticks, carefully fill in the room between the roots

The compost is smoothed over with a brush. Small pieces of moss can then be laid on the top of it

After repotting, the tree is watered adequately but with care so that the compost is not washed away

bowl. The Japanese never place a bonsai exactly in the centre of the bowl, as they have an aversion not only to even numbers but also to symmetry.

The surface of the compost is shaped so that it is gently heaped up towards the base of the trunk, giving a natural effect. In order to prevent the compost being washed away when watering, small pieces of moss are placed on it. The newly potted bonsai should be placed in a shady spot away from the wind and only after a month should feeding be resumed.

Compost mixtures

Ready-mixed bonsai compost is obtainable in specialist shops. However, it is possible to mix it oneself. The *Basic Mixture 1* consists of equal quantities of peat, loam and coarse sand. For young plants or deciduous trees, only a little loam is required, as these little plants want a light soil. Slower growing trees, such as pines and many conifers, or older trees want drier soil. These, then, simply require more sand in the soil mixture. *Basic Mixture 2* for coniferous trees consists of two parts sand and one part peat and one part loam.

Naturally, every bonsai specialist has his own special mixture by which he swears, but they all contain the same components in roughly the same proportions. The loam has a buffer effect, peat contains important humus elements, and sand takes care of aeration and drainage, preventing a build-up of moisture which bonsai cannot take.

Two more special tips:

In order to ensure that azalea bonsai have the required acid soil, the amount of peat is increased. For every two parts of loam and sand, mix in five of peat. With older deciduous trees the amount of peat in the basic recipe should be reduced somewhat so that they do not grow so much.

Cushions of moss and other plants for background effects

The addition of moss to the background planting and the tree conveys the impression of a landscape. It is not so difficult to maintain a covering of moss. It will grow on its own in the open after six to eight months under sufficiently damp conditions.

If this takes too long for you, there are other methods of planting moss. Moss grows all over the place in cracks, in walls, the edge of roofs, and in damp places. Such moss can be placed in small pieces onto the bonsai compost. Moss from the woods is not suitable as it grows too high.

An alternative to moss is to rub dried pieces of moss and then scatter them over the soil.

A ground cover of moss is not just beautiful, providing as it does a colourful contrast to the bonsai, it also has the advantage of holding the moisture longer in the soil and this means less watering. In addition, moss holds the soil together and prevents it from being washed away. Because it holds water, the moss must not be allowed to grow up the trunk, otherwise the plant will begin to rot.

The cushion of moss can be broken up by inter-plantings, for example, ferns, wild alpine violets and shrubs.

Watering

The art of watering lies in the right amount. A bonsai should be kept only slightly damp. The drainage holes in the bowl and a well draining compost mixture should ensure it does not get too wet. In summer especially, the bonsai needs regular watering, because a thin layer of earth dries out quickly. But in the dormancy of winter the little tree needs much less moisture.

Principally, the amount of water is dependant on the time of year, the temperature and the humidity.

Rain water or soft, possibly decalcified water is ideal. Mains water should stand for two or three days so that all chlorine is expelled and the water temperature stabilised.

A watering can with a very fine rose prevents the soil being washed away. Water the bonsai several times until, despite the shallow bowl, it receives enough water and is thoroughly soaked. In summer it is best to water in the morning and late afternoon as the hot midday sun would burn the tender damp leaves. If you are away for a long time, e.g. on holiday, ask someone to look after your tree, preferably a bonsai enthusiast or your specialist bonsai dealer.

Feeding

Water is not sufficient as a source of food for a bonsai to remain strong and healthy. For this reason it needs feeding from spring to autumn. Exceptions: freshly repotted plants and sick bonsai whose roots are not able to absorb the feed.

Feed organically with bonemeal, hoof and horn, and fishmeal. Japanese experts prefer organic fertiliser in pellet form which is also obtainable here. It contains a totally sufficient composition of organic fertilisers.

These pellets are placed halfway between the trunk and the edge of the bowl and dissolve slowly when watering. When they are gone, they are replaced by new pellets – the last ones at the end of August. For small bowls, about 10 cm wide and 15 cm in length, only one pellet is required, for middle sized (20 cm x 15 cm) two pellets, and for the large (40 cm x 30 cm), around four pellets.

If you prefer to use liquid feed, the instructions for use with pot plants should be followed. It is important before feeding bonsai to water them well.

Deciduous trees are fed from the time they sprout to when they shed their leaves in autumn. Conifers are fed until about the middle of October.

A Chinese elm in an informal upright style

Pages 106 and 107: stewartia – false camellia –
is particularly suitable for a miniature deciduous forest

Position

The Japanese have always placed their bonsai in an area somewhere between the garden and the house, but in any case outside in the open. Translating that into our own climate would mean a balcony, terrace or roof garden, or a garden near the house. Every bonsai needs normal weather conditions such as sun, wind and rain if it is not to get sick. It is and always remains a tree used to growing outside.

Most bonsai prefer a sunny situation – they are best in a raised position where they can be seen. Another point to be remembered is that raised on a stand they are in less danger from pets or pests. On a balcony a shelf is a good idea, perhaps along the parapet as the trees look particularly beautiful against the sky. Maples like a shady spot away from draughts.

The more beautiful the bonsai, the greater will be the temptation to bring it indoors as a decoration for guests to admire. But remember that it can only last a few days indoors without being harmed. If you are a bonsai enthusiast without a balcony or a garden, you should specialise in bonsai suitable for growing indoors as in the section on indoor bonsai (see p22). If a bonsai is standing on a balcony with only one side to the sun, it should be turned round every few weeks.

Overwintering

Many plant lovers view the onset of winter with its dangers from frost with mixed feelings. The overwintering of trees is not so difficult. The best thing is to keep them in a temperature of 0°–5°C in a bright and airy greenhouse.

Understandably, not everyone has the use of a greenhouse – but it is possible to overwinter in greenhouse 'substitutes'. Depending on the frost-sensitivity of the plants they must be looked after a little differently. With bonsai one must distinguish between winter-hardy varieties, half-hardy and frost-sensitive varieties.

Frost-sensitive bonsai plants, such as box, myrtle or

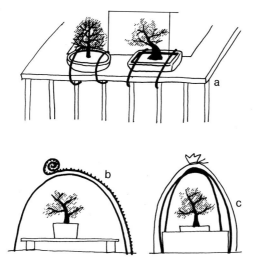

a) Balcony site: the bonsai dishes must be fastened with wire.
b) In summer, most deciduous bonsai should be lightly shaded.
c) In winter, the bonsai should be stood in a box of moist peat and be covered by polyethene stretched over a framework.

pomegranate, need a light, unheated place such as a bright stairway, storeroom or conservatory. The temperature must not rise above 8°C otherwise the plants will start to sprout. Spraying with water twice a week should provide the tree with sufficient humidity. In order to prevent the plant from drying out, the soil should be kept slightly damp.

Half-hardy varieties, such as sageretia, trident maple and cypress, will withstand temperatures down to −5°C. It is possible to construct winter protection oneself (see *hardy varieties*) to cover the coldest times in the year, and it is a good idea to install a warm lamp.

Hardy varieties can stay outside, but must be protected. Besides this, from September they should no longer be taken inside the house even for a short period so that when the frost starts they are already hardened.

The hardy varieties, such as beech, pines and juniper, appreciate overwintering in a home-made polythene house. Fill a box with damp peat or sand and sink the bonsai into it until just over the edge of the bowl. Now make a framework out of

The most important bonsai tools and accessories, from right to left.
Top row: mesh for covering the drainage holes, root cutters, leaf trimmers, brush, tweezers, branch shears, claws for pulling roots apart
Middle row: bonsai shears, narrow bonsai shears, small wire cutters, wire-removing pliers, wire cutters
Below: aluminium wire and small saw

wires, or bamboo canes stuck into the corners forming a frame, over which a polythene sheet can be stretched. To keep the polythene in place the ends can be tucked in under the box. In fine weather the polythene can be rolled back for ventilation. It is important that the bonsai are not exposed to great variations in temperature.

Bonsai tools

As is to be expected, the Japanese have developed tools for bonsai over a long period of time; they are the best to use when caring for plants. At first the bonsai enthusiast who is just beginning makes do with tools at hand. But before long problems inevitably arise, as for example with broom style, when the inner branches cannot be reached without damaging the outer ones. There are special narrow shears for this purpose. To add to this there are pliers for removing the wire without damaging the bark, and special cutters for removing branches. These leave a concave cut that heals quickly without leaving a scar.

If the tools are handled carefully and cleaned regularly they will provide many years of useful service.

Page 112: Needle juniper — formal upright style

RECOGNITION AND CONTROL
OF PESTS AND DISEASES

THE BEST protection against disease and pests is proper care and attention, and control of the plant's environment. Also, a good position will protect the bonsai from pests like snails, ants, caterpillars, etc. They should therefore never be grown directly in the ground.

Bonsai fall prey to the same pests and diseases as other house and garden plants. Should disease appear that is not a direct result of faulty care of the plant and is not in the area of the leaves, then the plant should be moved from its container. If the roots have strong white tips, one can be certain that the root system is all right and the symptoms have another cause.

Pesticides available in the shops for dealing with diseases in house plants can be used at the dosage prescribed, but under no circumstances should it be increased.

Pests

Now to the most important pests to which bonsai fall prey and the pesticides to deal with them. Remember, avoid spraying chemicals on newly opened leaves as this may harm them. Try washing the pests off with water in this instance.

Greenfly and *blackfly* are mostly found on shoots and the underside of leaves, but can almost always be removed by spraying with water to which has been added washing-up liquid. If this does not work, spray with malathion.

Scale insects spend most of their lifespan on the underside of leaves or on the branches and trunk of the plant. They appear as tiny limpet-like swellings that tend to remain in the same spot. They can be removed with a cotton wool bud or brush dipped in methylated spirits. Alternatively, spray with malathion or permethrin.

This Japanese quince in full blossom is some 75 years old and 65 cm high

This Japanese white pine is about 125 years old and has a height of 68 cm

Woolly aphids and *mealy bugs* look very similar at first glance as both are covered in a protective whitish wool. They infect twigs and branches. The creatures sit well protected because spray bounces off the woolly covering. Spray regularly with malathion or with a systemic insecticide.

Root aphids inhabit the soil and check growth. They cause the leaves to go yellow and then die. The white to grey aphids sit in the roots. They must not be confused with the white deposit to be found on pine roots. This is a fungus which lives in symbiosis with the pine and is a sign of health, not disease. The fungus-type smell is easily recognised. A plant attacked by root aphids can be treated by drenching the root system with diazinon spray.

Red spider mite – settles mainly in dry years in many conifers such as juniper, black pine and firs, but can also cause a lot of damage to deciduous trees. The mites cause the needles and leaves to go speckled yellow and pale. Sometimes only a few branches of the plant are affected. Under a magnifying glass the mites can be spotted easily if the infected branches are shaken over a sheet of white paper, when they can be seen moving on the paper. Depending on the stage of development and what they have been eating, the mites can be coloured red, yellow or light brown. They like dry conditions, so regular spraying with water discourages them. Malathion spray will also help to control them.

Caterpillars are the larval stages of moths or butterflies, and several of them are pests. Most feed on leaves, though some species live in the soil and attack roots. You may find caterpillars distorting the leaves of your bonsai by attaching several together with sticky webs. Remove them by hand and spray with malathion as a precaution against any others you may have missed.

Slugs and snails. Damage from feeding snails can be recognised by the slime trails left behind. They can be disposed of by slug pellets laid in the evening near the bonsai.

Diseases

Amongst the main diseases are:

Powdery mildew is a fungus found as a white mealy coating on leaf surfaces. It can appear any time during the year, especially in spring and autumn when it is damp. Access to a fair amount of nitrogen will encourage this fungus. To eradicate it use a fungicide containing benomyl or propiconazole.

Grey mould (botrytis) can be identified by blotchiness of the leaves and fluffy greyish growth on leaves and stems. When these symptoms appear, remove the dead leaves and put the tree in a well ventilated place. Spray with benomyl.

Chlorosis shows itself when the leaves or needles turn yellow, whilst the leaf veins remain green. The main cause of this condition is lack of iron. This is most common in acid-loving plants if there is too much alkalinity in the soil, e.g. azaleas and rhododendrons. This damage can be remedied by mixing plenty of peat into the soil and applying chelated iron. Only acid fertilisers should be used.

Compacted, damp earth can also cause yellowing of the leaves as the plant in this case does not receive enough oxygen. The remedy is to loosen the earth, or possibly repot and water less.

Rust is a fungal disease, and looks like dark brown or orange spots. It occurs on the older leaves. Destroy all infected material and treat with propiconazole.

Root rot is a disease very commonly met and can have a number of different causes. First signs of root rot are that the leaves go brown and complete branches die off. The plants become weak and die. Root rot occurs because of faulty care and attention, such as too much watering, overfeeding or a wrong compost mixture. Also, in periods of drought the fine root-hairs may die and then rot when watered.

By the time symptoms appear, the tree may be beyond saving. But first try removing all the rotten roots and then the

remaining root system must be treated with benomyl and the tree re-planted in fresh compost. It is important to water sparingly as the root-hairs must first regrow and the plant will not be able to take up so much water as a completely healthy one. Spray the bonsai more often. In addition, the tree should be kept in the shade and away from draughts. A plant that has suffered root damage can only be given feed again when it has grown sufficient new roots.

Whenever problems arise, turn to your local specialist dealer for advice. Go earlier rather than later to a specialist – better too often than too late.

Chinese bonsai: a bizarre style

BONSAI CARE AND TRAINING

Winter-hardy means that the plant can stand frost. As mentioned on p109, the bonsai should be protected from frost despite this. Half-hardy means that the plant can stand a few degrees of frost, up to −5°C, and therefore should be kept free from frost, at 0°−8°C, over winter. Frost-tender plants should be overwintered at 4°−6°C.

Species	Description	Pruning the branches	Pruning the shoots	Wiring
Acer buergerianum Trident maple	Deciduous tree with triple-lobed leaves turning bright red, orange and purple in the autumn	February-March before sprouting; small branches in September again	May-September. Continually cut back to 1–3 pairs of leaves	March or June, after cutting the leaves
Acer palmatum 'Atropurpureum' Japanese mountain maple	Deciduous tree with glowing red shoots and red autumn colours	February–March before sprouting; fine branches also in September	After sprouting. In September, shorten to 1–3 pairs of leaves.	March or in June after cutting the leaves
Betula nigra Birch	Very beautiful deciduous tree with a white trunk, fresh green leaves and catkins in spring	March-April before sprouting	Take back shoots to 1–2 eyes	June–July
Buxus microphylla Box	Evergreen, small-leaved bush or tree with a yellow-white bark	March–April before sprouting	Continually cut shoots back to 2–3 eyes	Always, except in extreme cold
Carpinus laxiflora Hornbeam	Deciduous tree with fine branches and very beautiful shoots in spring	March-April before sprouting	April–September, continually cut shoots back to 1–2 eyes	June–July
Chamaecyparis species False cypress	Evergreen conifers with scale-like leaves arranged in flattened sprays	March–April and September–October	Pinch back shoots continually to ⅔ until beginning of September	February–March, September–October

Watering: It is only possible to give very general instructions about watering. It is for you to discover how much water each of your plants requires. This will depend on temperature, humidity, and the condition of the plant. During sprouting, watering should be reduced (see p104).

Repotting	Position	Hardiness	Watering	Feeding	PH
Before sprouting of young plants every 1-2 years, older trees every 2-3 years	In high summer, light shadow	Limited hardiness	Generous	After sprouting, pellet feeding or liquid every 4 weeks	5.5-5.8
Before sprouting, young plants every 1-2 years, older plants every 2-3 years	In high summer, light shadow	Limited hardiness	Generous	After sprouting, pellet feeding or liquid every 4 weeks	5.5-5.8
Before sprouting every 2 years	Full sun	Hardy	Less	April-September, every 4 weeks liquid feed or pellets	4.8-5.5
Before sprouting every 2 years	Withstands full sun and shade	Limited hardiness	Generous	April-September, every 4 weeks liquid feed or pellets	5.5-6.0
Before sprouting, young trees every 2 years, older trees every 3-5 years	Full sun, good ventilation	Hardy	Generous	After sprouting, every 4 weeks until September	5.8-6.0
March-May every 2 years	Light shadow	Hardy	Generous	April-October every 4 weeks	5.5-5.8

Species	Description	Pruning the branches	Pruning the shoots.	Wiring
Cotoneaster species	Evergreen and deciduous varieties in different shapes. Beautiful bright berries	March–April before sprouting	Take back in June to 2–3 eyes. Shorten longer shoots in September	Always
Cupressus sempervirens Cypress	Evergreen, quick-growing, upright trees with scale-like leaves	In spring before sprouting	Pinch out shoots continually until beginning of September up to ⅔	February-March September–October
Cryptomeria japonica Japanese cedar	Evergreen conifer. Autumn colouring red to dark brown, fresh green in spring	February–March	Pinch out shoots continually until beginning of September up to ⅔	February-March September–October
Fagus sylvatica 'Purpurea Pendula' Weeping purple beech	Strong, deciduous with thin green leaves that turn brown in autumn	March–April before sprouting, or September	Take back shoots in May-June to 2–3 eyes	July–July and autumn
Ficus species Fig	Evergreen, tropical deciduous tree. Small-leaved species are well suited to bonsai	Continually	Take back shoots continually to 2–3 leaves	Always, but only for three months at a time
Gardenia jasminoides	Evergreen shrub with shiny oval leaves and strongly scented blossom	March–April before sprouting	When blossoming is over, take back all shoots to 2–3 pairs of leaves. In July, cut back to 2–3 eyes	June–July
Ginkgo biloba Maidenhair tree	The oldest tree on earth, going back 200 million years, deciduous, with fern-like leaves	March–April before sprouting	Shorten shoots on young plants to 4–5 leaves, on older plants to 1–2	June–July and autumn

Repotting	Position	Hardiness	Watering	Feeding	PH
Before the sprouting, in young plants every 1–2 years, older plants every 3–4 years	Full sun	Hardy	Generous	After sprouting, until October every 14 days	5.5–5.8
March–May, every 2 years	Full sun	Protect from frost	Generous	May–October, every 4 weeks	5.5–5.8
March–May, every 2 years	Full sun	Limited hardiness	Generous	April–October, every 4 weeks	5.5–5.8
Before sprouting, young plants every 1–2 years, older plants every 3–5 years	Full sun	Hardy	Generous	After sprouting, until end of September every 4 weeks	5.8–6.0
In spring every 3 years	Indoors, not under 18°C	Protect from frost	Less	April–August every 4 weeks	5.5–6.0
Before sprouting in spring, every 2 years	Half shadow or indoors	Protect from frost	Generous	April until end September every 4 weeks	5.8–6.0
Before sprouting in spring, young plants every 1–2 years, older plants every 3–5 years	Full sun	Hardy	Generous	April until end September every 4 weeks	5.8–6.0

Species	Description	Pruning the branches	Pruning the shoots	Wiring
Jasminum nudiflorum Winter-flowering jasmine	Deciduous bush with overhanging branches and yellow blossom in winter	March–April	After flowering, cut back every shoot to 1–2 eyes. In July take new shoots back to 2–3 eyes	June–July
Juniperus chinensis Chinese juniper	The species is conic in shape, but there are dwarf and spreading forms. Slow growing	March–April, September–October	Pinch out shoots by ⅔ continually until the beginning of September	September–October February–March
Juniperus rigida Needle juniper, temple juniper	Evergreen conifer with very prickly awl-shaped leaves	February–March	Pinch back shoots continually by ½ until beginning of September	September–October February–March
Larix decidua Larch	Graceful conifer of straight, upright growth. Grows quickly when young. Needles become gold in autumn, then drop	March–April before sprouting	Take back shoots to 2 needle whorls from June to September	September–October February–March
Malus species and varieties Crab apple	Attractive deciduous trees, several of which are suitable for bonsai. They bear blossom ranging from white and pale pink to deep red-purple	March–April before sprouting	Take back shoots in June to 1–2 cm, in September long shoots back to 1 cm	June–July
Picea species Fir, spruce	Robust, evergreen conifers, mainly with a narrow pyramidical shape. Some dwarf forms are in cultivation	February–March, October	Let new shoots grow until July to 2 cm, then cut back to 0.5–1 cm	October–March

Repotting	Position	Hardiness	Watering	Feeding	PH
After blossom, March–April or September–October every 2 years	Full sun	Hardy	Generous	March–October every 6 weeks	5.8–6.0
Before sprouting every 2 years	Full sun	Hardy	Generous	April–October every 4 weeks	5.8–6.0
Before sprouting every 2 years	Full sun	Hardy	Generous	April–October every 4 weeks	5.8–6.0
Before sprouting every 2 years	Full sun	Hardy	Generous	April–October every 4 weeks	5.8–6.0
Yearly, in October	Full sun	Hardy	Generous	After blossom until September every 4 weeks	5.8–6.0
Before sprouting or in September every 2 years	Full sun, but in high summer in light shadow	Hardy	Generous	April-October every 4 weeks	5.8–6.0

Species	Description	Pruning the branches	Pruning the shoots	Wiring
Pinus Pine	Quick-growing, evergreen conifers. The leaves are needle-like and in groups of two, three or five to a sheath	February–March, October	Removes shoots completely in June/July	October-March
Pinus parviflora Japanese white pine	Slow-growing pine with short, blue–green needles in groups of five	February–March, October	Shorten candles before opening by ⅓ to ⅔ in May/June	October–March
Prunus mume Japanese apricot	Deciduous tree with white-pink blossom in January/February	After blossoming, in February–March	After blossoming, take-back all shoots to 2–3 eyes. In August, shorten tips of all shoots. In September, again cut back to 4–5 eyes	June, July
Prunus serrulata Japanese cherry	East Asian wild cherry, a deciduous tree with upright branches and brown bark. White-pink blossoms end April-May	After blossoming, in March–April	After the blossoming, take back all shoots to 2 eyes, new shoots then back to 2–3 eyes	June, July
Pyracantha species and varieties Firethorn	Evergreen, thorny shrubs with white blossom in summer and red, orange or yellow winter berries	Before sprouting, March–April	Take back shoots in May to 2 eyes. In September, shorten shoots that are too long	June, July
Zelkova serrata Zelkova	Deciduous tree with upright trunk, long splayed branches and small, oval, ridged leaves	March–April, before sprouting	Cut back shoots continually to 1–3 eyes until September	June, August and spring before sprouting

Repotting	Position	Hardiness	Watering	Feeding	PH
Before sprouting or in September every 2–3 years	Full sun	Hardy	Less	April–October every 4 weeks	5.8–6.0
Before sprouting or in September every 2–3 years	Full sun	Hardy	Less	April–October every 4 weeks	5.8–6.0
After blossoming every 1–2 years	Full sun	Limited hardiness	Less	March–June every 4 weeks	5.8–6.0
After the blossoming, every 1–2 years	Full sun	Hardy	Less	After blossoming, May–September every 4 weeks	5.8–6.0
Before sprouting in spring every 2 years	Full sun	Hardy	Generous	May to end September every 4 weeks, except during blossoming	5.8
Before sprouting, young plants every 2 years, older plants every 3–4 years	Full sun	Limited hardiness	Generous	After sprouting, until September every 4 weeks or pellets	5.5–5.8

These unusual looking plants belong to the Bromeliad plant family, as does the pineapple. They are indigenous to Mexico, Central and South America. In nature, many of the tillandsias grow on trees as epiphytes, or air plants. Their roots are used mainly for support. They are not parasitic and some grow on rocks or cliffs. All moisture and food is absorbed through the leaves. They are remarkably versatile and their diverse forms compose one of the most adaptable plant families in the world.

HUMIDITY/AIR: High humidity and good air circulation are essential. Localized humidity in the house can be increased by grouping plants together and misting the area frequently.

WATERING: Mist leaves thoroughly once a week, more often when hot and dry.

LIGHT: Bright diffuse light is required. Stiff, thick leafed, and greyish-white types can take bright light intensity. Green, soft leaf types do best with lowered light intensity.

TEMPERATURE: Tillandsias will generally tolerate a broad range of temperature between 35 and 110 degrees F. However, they are not winter hardy except in tropical regions.

FERTILIZER: The easiest way to fertilize is to put 2 to 3 drops of any liquid fertilizer into a small spray bottle, and use this whenever misting the plants. Fertilize from Spring through Fall; it is not necessary to fertilize in the winter months.

BLOOMING: All of these tillandsias will only bloom once in their lifetimes. All blooms are different and attractive. Some of the plants will change the color of their leaves from subdued green to bright red just before they begin to bloom, and then return to green after blooming. Blooms may last anywhere from 6 weeks to 6 months depending on the species and conditions.

PUPS & OFFSETS: After the plant has bloomed, it will slowly die over the next year or two. HOWEVER, the plant will replace itself with new plants called pups, or offsets. Most of the pups grow off the mother plant at the base. Some grow on stolens. Continue to care for your mounted tillandsia as always, and allow the pup to grow to maturity. It too will bloom within another year. When the mother plant begins to look like it is dying, and the pups are at least half as big as the parent, you can trim the leaves with scissors near the base of each leaf. This will allow room for the new pups to grow and begin yet another generation of plants for your enjoyment.